# GLOBETR...

## *Travel*

...y Helms
6223 Trotter Rd.
Clarksville, MD 21029

# LONDON

## NICK HANNA
### UPDATED BY CAROL SYKES

NEW
HOLLAND

NEW
HOLLAND

> ★★★ Highly recommended
> ★★ Recommended
> ★ See if you can

This edition published in 2001
by New Holland Publishers (UK) Ltd
London • Cape Town • Sydney • Auckland
First published in 1997
10 9 8 7 6 5 4 3 2 1

Garfield House, 86 Edgware Road, London W2 2EA
United Kingdom

80 McKenzie Street, Cape Town 8001
South Africa

14 Aquatic Drive, Frenchs Forest NSW2086
Australia

218 Lake Road, Northcote, Auckland
New Zealand

Copyright © 2001 in text: Nick Hanna
Copyright © 2001 in maps: Globetrotter Travel Maps
Copyright © 2001 in photographs:
Individual photographers as credited
Copyright © 1997, 1999, 2001 New Holland
Publishers (UK) Ltd

ISBN  1 85974 769 8

Consultant: Peter Matthews (1999)
Commissioning Editor: Tim Jollands
Manager Globetrotter Maps: John Loubser
Managing Editors: Thea Grobbelaar, Sean Fraser
Editors: Nic Orfang, Catherine Mallinick, Gill
Gordon, Rowena Curtis
Design and DTP: Lellyn Creamer, Sonya Cupido,
John Loubser
Cartographers: Nicole Engeler, William Smuts,
Éloïse Moss
Compiler/Verifier: Elaine Fick
Proofreader: Ingrid Schneider

Reproduction by Hirt & Carter (Pty) Ltd, Cape Town
Printed and bound in Hong Kong by Sing Cheong
Printing Co. Ltd.

Cover: British Airways London Eye.
Title Page: Westminster by night.

# CONTENTS

# 1
# Introducing London

'When a man is tired of London he is tired of life', wrote Samuel Johnson – a sentiment which is no less true today than it was in the 18th century. It is one of the great capitals of the world, the largest city in Europe, and the central focus of politics, the arts, entertainment, the media, the judiciary and much else in Britain itself.

For the visitor, London offers an endless pageant of history and tradition combined with the excitement of the avant-garde, a dizzying variety of entertainment, innumerable sporting events, a surprising number of parks and green spaces, culinary offerings that encompass almost every cuisine under the sun, and, of course, a vast selection of shops.

The well-known highlights – such as the Tower of London, Buckingham Palace, St Paul's Cathedral and other major monuments – attract scores of tour buses, but London also has many hidden corners which repay exploration, characterful backstreets which evoke the London of Charles Dickens, wonderful riverside or canal walks, unusual speciality museums, and tranquil Georgian squares.

Like any big city, London has its problems – traffic jams and pollution, litter, and a growing number of the dispossessed and homeless – and the weather may not be the best in the world, but it still manages to extend a warm welcome to its 25 million annual visitors. London is a place which everyone has to visit at least once in their lifetime – it is one of the most dynamic, vibrant and exciting cities in the world.

---

**TOP ATTRACTIONS**

**\*\*\* British Museum:** the city's most popular attraction.
**\*\*\*London Eye:** spectacular bird's-eye view of London
**\*\*\* The National Gallery:** one of the world's most important art collections.
**\*\*\* Tower of London:** living history in this medieval fortress.
**\*\*\* St Paul's Cathedral:** an enduring symbol in the heart of the city.
**\*\*\* South Kensington museums:** the city's finest.
**\*\*\* Westminster Abbey:** resting place of the monarchs.
**\*\*Madame Tussaud's:** waxworks extravaganza.

---

**Opposite:** *The stately Royal Carriages leave Buckingham Palace.*

## THE LAND

In geological terms, most of the southeast of England is relatively young and dates back to between 135 and 70 million years ago. London itself lies mostly over sand and clay (in the north) and chalk and flint (in the south). Its defining geographical feature is the **River Thames**, which bisects the city and flows out via the Thames Estuary to the North Sea.

**Above:** *Running through the heart of London, the River Thames has always played a crucial role in the city's history.*

### The Thames

In prehistoric times the 16km (10 mile) wide **Thames Valley** offered fertile soils, extensive woodlands and a plentiful water supply to the early settlers. The core of the city, dating back to Roman times, developed at the point nearest the mouth of the Thames, where it was both feasible to build bridges and to anchor large ships in deep water. The Thames is a **tidal** river, and extensive areas on either side of its banks are classified as flood plains. In Roman times, areas to the south of the river (such as today's Lambeth and Southwark) were swampy marshes and frequently inundated. Over the centuries the southeast of England has been gradually tilting towards the sea, and central London would still be subject to flooding from surge tides were it not for the recently built **Thames Barrier** (*see* p. 103).

London was the first capital in the world to experience the Industrial Revolution, and the banks of the Thames are crammed with vestiges of the city's heyday as the centre of the British Empire.

### Climate

London has a temperate climate, with the prevailing southwesterlies creating predominantly damp conditions. It's almost impossible to generalize about the weather in London, since it is highly changeable (perhaps this is why the weather always seems to feature so prominently in

**THAMES TRIPS**

Although the Thames's role is not as pivotal as it once was, exploring the riverside history of London is a great pleasure. The main wharves for river cruises are at the Tower of London, Embankment (Charing Cross) and West-minster, but there are others. Regular services run down-river to Greenwich all year and on to the Thames Barrier in summer, with extended sailings in the summer upriver from Westminster to Kew, Richmond and Hampton Court. There are also lunch and dinner cruises. Details can be obtained by calling the (premium rate) Vistorcall number for river trips, tel: (09068) 505 471 or picking up the free 'Thames river cruises' booklet.

| LONDON | J | F | M | A | M | J | J | A | S | O | N | D |
|---|---|---|---|---|---|---|---|---|---|---|---|---|
| AVERAGE TEMP. °F | 40 | 40 | 44 | 49 | 55 | 61 | 64 | 64 | 59 | 52 | 46 | 42 |
| AVERAGE TEMP. °C | 5 | 5 | 7 | 10 | 13 | 16 | 18 | 18 | 15 | 12 | 8 | 6 |
| HOURS OF SUN DAILY | 1.5 | 2.2 | 3.7 | 5.3 | 6.6 | 7.1 | 6.6 | 6.2 | 4.7 | 3.2 | 1.7 | 1.3 |
| RAINFALL ins. | 2.1 | 1.6 | 1.5 | 1.5 | 1.8 | 1.8 | 2.2 | 2.3 | 1.9 | 2.2 | 3 | 1.9 |
| RAINFALL mm | 54 | 40 | 37 | 37 | 46 | 45 | 57 | 59 | 49 | 57 | 64 | 48 |
| DAYS OF RAINFALL | 15 | 13 | 11 | 12 | 12 | 11 | 12 | 11 | 13 | 13 | 15 | 15 |

locals' conversations). Global climatic changes also seem to be having an impact, with unseasonal winter storms on the one hand and near-drought over the summer months on the other contributing to the unpredictability of weather forecasting. **Spring** (March, April, May) is generally a pleasant time to visit, although cold March winds and April showers can dampen the days; **summer** (June, July, August) often sees sweltering hot days (or weeks) followed by thunderstorms and overcast skies; **autumn** (September, October, November) can vary from hot, summer-like days in September to crisp, clear weather in October, with November traditionally one of the wettest months; **winter** (December, January, February) is a season you should come well prepared for, with cold conditions and rain, hail, sleet or even snow a possibility.

## Plant Life

London's parks, squares and public gardens are home to a huge variety of plant life. In the Royal Parks stately oaks and other trees date back hundreds of years. **St James's Park**, east of Buckingham Palace, is one such, with a pleasing mix of hawthorn, plane and lime trees and a weeping willow alongside the lake. **Regent's Park**, by contrast, is known for its displays of colourful flower borders. **Hyde Park** and **Kensington Gardens** offer a variety of trees, flowers and shrubberies, with

**Below:** *St James's Park with Horse Guards Parade. In spring, the park is a riot of colour with white and purple crocuses.*

### WETLAND CENTRE, BARNES

Across the Thames from Hammersmith (special Duck Bus from Hammersmith tube – or ordinary bus No.283) were the London reservoirs. When they became obsolete, conservationists created a wetland reserve. Combining special habitats with a large wildlife area has provided a haven for 130 species of bird (some on the verge of extinction). Strategically positioned hides, 'Field Notes', interactive games and a visitor centre with an excellent café are available. Open daily at 9:30, closing 16:00 or later (up to 20:30).

**Below:** *A fallow deer buck in Richmond Park, one of London's wildlife havens.*

daffodils lining busy Park Lane during spring. **Battersea Park**, south of the river, features blooming cherry and acacia in the spring. **Richmond Park** in southwest London is renowned for its magnificent oak trees, as well as thickets of flowering rhododendrons. For plant lovers London's main Mecca is, of course, the wonderful **Royal Botanic Gardens** at Kew, where greenhouses contain everything from towering palms and epiphytes to climbers and sacred lotus plants. One of the greatest storehouses in the world for plants of all kinds, Kew has magnificent displays (*see* p. 109).

## Wildlife

London has a surprising variety of birdlife, even though in many areas all you see are pigeons, sparrows and starlings. The parks are home to numerous species, many of them introduced. The Serpentine in Hyde Park, for instance, is a fishing ground for tufted ducks, mallards, great crested grebes, moorhens, coots, and herons. In spring, migrant birds such as willow warblers, redstarts and spotted flycatchers are often seen in the parks' woodlands. Grey squirrels (introduced from North America) are fairly ubiquitous too. The largest of the royal parks, Richmond, is home to kestrels, great spotted woodpeckers, nuthatches and other bird species, as well as deer (*see* p. 110).

Once so polluted that nothing could live in it, the Thames has been cleaned up and fish have started to recolonize it. Blackheaded, common and herring gulls may be seen dipping in it as they fish, and along the more rural areas upstream the kingfisher is in evidence as are elegant swans (protected for centuries as Crown property). The Thames Estuary and the new Wetland Centre (*see* box) are important habitats for migrating birds during the winter months.

# HISTORY IN BRIEF

The Thames Valley was home to hunter-gatherers some 500,000 years ago, and although there were isolated settlements by the time of the **Celts** it was not until the arrival of the **Romans** that a larger, more permanent settlement was founded.

## Londinium to Lundenwic

In AD43 an invasion force of four Roman legions sailed from Boulogne, landing at Richborough in Kent and overwhelming the Celtic forces along the way before building a pontoon bridge across the Thames (probably near present-day Westminster) to push further northwards. Their goal was the powerful tribal stronghold of Camulodunum (Colchester), which, once conquered, became the Roman capital.

In AD60 a major rebellion by the **Iceni** tribes, under **Queen Boudicca** (Boadicea), led to the sacking of Camulodunum and a massacre of the inhabitants of the river crossing at **Londinium**. After the defeat of the Iceni (and Boudicca's suicide) Londinium was rebuilt as the main Roman base in Britain. The port prospered and grew to become the fifth most important city in the Roman Empire until the withdrawal of the Romans in the 5th century AD.

During the 6th century the settlement – then known as **Lundenwic** – prospered once more under the Anglo-Saxons, and became a thriving port until being razed to the ground by the **Vikings** in AD851. Some 30 years later the English, led by King Alfred the Great, recaptured London, but by 1016 it had again fallen to the Danes.

The death of pious (and celibate) **Edward the Confessor** – who founded Westminster Abbey – in 1066, was soon followed by the invasion of **William the Conqueror**, who laid the foundations for the Tower of London and Windsor Castle. London's special status was reaffirmed by the election of its first **mayor** in the 12th century.

**Above:** *The statue of Queen Boudicca at Westminster, a reminder of London's Roman past.*

### GEOFFREY CHAUCER

Born into a family of London vintners, poet **Geoffrey Chaucer** (c. 1342–1400) travelled widely in his many jobs – he was at various times a diplomat, customs official, member of parliament and a soldier – and the wide range of people he met contributed to his great knowledge of human nature, which was expounded to such good effect in *The Canterbury Tales*. This rollicking saga of pilgrims on the road to Canterbury was one of the first books to be printed and the first major work of literature in the English language.

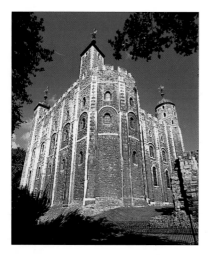

## The Middle Ages

By the 14th century London's population had reached around 80,000 people but the **Black Death** (1348) wiped out over a third of the population. Economic unrest led to the **Peasant's Revolt** of 1381, a protest at the imposition of the poll tax in which Londoners opened their gates to the rebels (under Wat Tyler) and joined in the ransacking of palaces and merchants' houses.

Throughout the 15th century trade with other countries continued to expand, and the wharfs around **London Bridge** were stacked high with cargo such as wines, spices, furs, and imported cloth. Literacy was on the increase and in 1476 **William Caxton** returned from Bruges with the first printing press, which he set up at Westminster. He published over 90 books (including an edition of *The Canterbury Tales*) before his death, after which his assistant Wynkyn de Worde moved his presses to the Fleet Street district, establishing the beginnings of the printing and publishing trade in the area which was to last for several centuries.

## Tudors and Stuarts

With the defeat of Richard III by Henry VII in the **Wars of the Roses**, the House of Tudor established a long-lasting peace, during which London became a centre for world commerce, with the opening up of trade routes to the Orient and the discovery of America. During the reign of **Henry VIII** the Royal Navy was established and the Church of England split from Rome – the **Reformation**, as it was known, was instigated by the king, who wanted to divorce his first wife, Catherine of Aragon. During the Dissolution of the Monasteries (1536) which followed, scores of churches and monasteries in the capital were ransacked; many were then converted to secular use by the Tudor nobility.

---

### ELIZABETHAN THEATRE

The 'golden age' of the Elizabethan era led to the flowering of literature and drama and the rise of play-wrights and authors such as William Shakespeare, Ben Jonson and Christopher Marlowe. Theatre performances took place on temporary stages outside pubs, and were looked down upon by the city fathers as degenerate. James Burbage then constructed London's first theatre in Shoreditch, outside the City boundaries, in 1574. Later, he dismantled it to create the **Globe** in Southwark (*see* p. 97), where Shakespeare's plays were first performed. The Globe has now been recreated, albeit not on the original site.

Henry VIII built a new palace, **St James's**, seized **Hampton Court** from his former chancellor, Thomas Wolsey, and established numerous hunting areas which are today London's Royal Parks: Hyde Park, Regent's Park, Richmond Park and Greenwich Park.

Under **Elizabeth I** the country enjoyed considerable prosperity, and the establishment of the city's first trading centre, the **Royal Exchange** (built by Sir Thomas Gresham in 1567), helped shift the balance of commercial power in Europe from Antwerp to London. The establishment of joint-stock companies (such as the Levant Company, Hudson Bay Company and East India Company) facilitated the exploits of seafarers and traders such as Walter Raleigh, Francis Drake and John Hawkins. By 1600 London had grown to encompass a population of around 200,000 people.

The Tudor dynasty ended in 1603 with the death of Elizabeth I. She was succeeded by James VI of Scotland, who united the two countries for the first time, becoming James I of England and VI of Scotland. The continued persecution of Catholics led to the **Gunpowder Plot** on 5 November 1605, when Guy Fawkes and his fellow conspirators were caught in the act of trying to blow up the Houses of Parliament in protest.

Under James I's son, Charles I, the Crown found itself at odds with Parliament and the City and tensions increased when the king tried (unsuccessfully) to arrest five Members of Parliament in 1642: this sparked a **Civil War** with the Royalists pitched against the Parliamentarians under Oliver Cromwell. The Royalists lost, and Charles I was executed outside the Banqueting House in Whitehall on 30 January 1649.

For the next 11 years England became a Republic under Oliver Cromwell, until the **Restoration** of the monarchy under Charles II in 1660.

In 1665, London was hit by an outbreak of the **bubonic plague**, and the following year another major disaster occurred when the **Great Fire** of 1666 destroyed large areas of the city (*see* p. 74); it did, however, wipe out the last remnants of the plague.

---

### THE PLAGUE

As London expanded, conditions became increasingly unsanitary: the Thames was not only the main highway and water supply, but also the main dumping ground for sewage and effluents from the tanning, brewing and soap industries. There were outbreaks of **bubonic plague** (carried by fleas living on black rats) in 1603, 1625, 1636 and 1647, but a long, hot summer in 1665 led to an epidemic which killed around 100,000 inhabitants of the city.

**Opposite:** *The White Tower is at the centre of the great medieval castle of the Tower of London.* **Below:** *Staple Inn in Holborn, one of the few timber-framed buildings to survive the Great Fire.*

Charles II wanted to reconstruct London along continental lines, with grand boulevards and circuses, but the intricacies of property ownership rendered this impractical. Many streets were, however, considerably widened as rebuilding went ahead – and bricks and mortar replaced the wooden houses of medieval London.

## Georgian London

In 1714 the throne passed to George of Hanover, who became **George I** but never learned to speak English. Parliament gained in stature and the leader of the Whigs (Liberals), Sir Robert Walpole, effectively became the first Prime Minister. The king presented him with **No. 10 Downing Street**, which has traditionally been the Prime Minister's residence ever since.

London continued to grow, and numerous Georgian-style squares and terraces were built in Soho, Bloomsbury, Marylebone and Mayfair. The **West End** was developed as a fashionable shopping area, but squalor and poverty were also on the increase. The **East End** saw considerable deprivation and appallingly high death rates – the latter particularly fuelled by a glut of cheap gin, consumed at the rate of around two pints per week by adults and children alike. In 1751, Parliament was

forced to raise the price of gin to try and halt the epidemic. The imbalance between the rich and the poor led to high crime rates – daylight robbery in the West End was not unknown – and an increasing number of riots, one of the most serious of which was the **Gordon Riots** of 1780, which lasted for five days and led to over 300 deaths.

## The 19th Century

In 1801, when the first official census was taken, London's population stood at around one million inhabitants, making it the most populous city in Europe. Over the next century it grew to nearly seven million as the city became increasingly industrialized and developed as the commercial and administrative hub of the British Empire. In 1811 the Prince Regent (later King George IV), laid out plans for Regent's Park and Regent Street with architect John Nash; the British Museum was begun in 1823, the National Gallery in 1824, and London University was founded in 1826.

**Above:** *Cumberland Terrace, in Regent's Park, is an elegant example of Nash architecture.*

**Opposite:** *Downing Street has been the residence of Prime Ministers since the mid 18th century.*

During the reign of **Queen Victoria**, roads, railways and houses continued to be built right across the capital, and docks were developed on the banks of the Thames. Pollution, squalor, prostitution and overcrowding were endemic in the slumlands of the East End; this was the underbelly of prosperous Victorian society which was so effectively chronicled by Charles Dickens.

The city's first railway line (from London Bridge to Greenwich) was opened in 1836, and the first under-ground line (between Paddington and Farringdon Road) was built in 1863. The achievements of the Victorian era were celebrated in the **Great Exhibition** (*see* p. 59) of 1851, an event which was so successful (attracting over six million visitors) that it led Prince Albert, the Queen's Consort, to establish an 'arts and science metropolis' – the foundation of today's museums in South Kensington.

### London at War

At the outbreak of **World War I** in August 1914 the crowds cheered the troops off to war, but the patriotic euphoria was short-lived as it became apparent that it was not going to be 'all over by Christmas'. The first bombs (dropped from a Zeppelin) fell on Stoke Newington in May 1915, but casualties in the capital were slight compared to the mortality rate and the horrors of the trenches in Belgium and northern France.

#### EDWARDIAN DECADENCE

The turn of the century in London was marked by the decadent Edwardian era, with flamboyant fashions and music halls enlivening the city after the dour Victorian years. The Ritz, Harrods, the Café Royal, Whiteleys and Selfridges opened for business, and the first motor cars were seen on the streets of the capital. Motor buses gradually replaced the horse-drawn variety, and electric trams were introduced.

**Above:** *The Map Room, one of the Cabinet War Rooms where Churchill and his Cabinet held meetings during World War II.*

In the inter-war years London's population continued to expand. The greatest growth was in the newly created suburbs, particularly to the north. The voting franchise was extended to all males over 21 years of age and females over 30, although it was not until 1928 that universal suffrage was achieved. Previously the vote had been restricted to the landed gentry, middle-class professionals, and 'settled tenants' (workers in towns).

In an attempt to emulate the success of the Great Exhibition, the British Empire Exhibition was held at Wembley in 1924–5, but its displays of the wealth and might of the Empire were overshadowed by a looming Depression. A confrontation between mine-owners and the unions led to the **General Strike** of 1926, with London in a state of near anarchy for nine days until the strike leaders caved in.

At the outbreak of **World War II** in 1939 trench shelters were dug in London's parks, over 600,000 women and children were evacuated to the countryside, and the strict enforcement of night-time blackouts led to a huge increase in road accidents. But the bombs didn't arrive for another year, with the beginning of the **Blitz** in September 1940, marked by many deaths and thousands injured.

## Postwar Years

Victory in Europe (VE) Day, in 1945, was followed by a General Election, where Winston Churchill was defeated by Clement Attlee's Labour Party. The Welfare State was created and the government embarked on wholesale nationalization of key industries. But in the capital the most pressing problem was a shortage of houses: prefabricated buildings were erected all over the city and massive high-rise housing estates were built on derelict bomb sites. In an attempt to relieve

### THE BLITZ

During the Blitz, the Luftwaffe bombed the capital for 57 consecutive nights, during which Londoners sought shelter in the underground stations or purpose-built shelters in their gardens. Firemen and thousands of volunteers fought bravely to contain the fires and rescue those buried in the rubble of their houses. The worst night came on 29 December 1940, when thousands of incendiary bombs threatened to set the capital alight. By the end of the Blitz, in May 1941, over a third of the City and the East End lay in ruins; over 30,000 people had died, with 50,000 injured and 130,000 houses destroyed.

the austerity of day-to-day life, the **Festival of Britain** was staged in 1951 on the south bank of the Thames; the site eventually became the South Bank Centre.

During the 1950s the population of the capital fell, although there was also a large influx of immigrants from the former colonies and the Caribbean. The '**Swinging Sixties**' heralded a new era of liberation and 'groovy' London became the music and fashion capital of the world.

The 1970s seemed drab by comparison, with economic austerity leading to the three-day week in 1974 and the downfall of the Conservative government. Britain became part of the EEC, and the IRA started a long bombing campaign on the mainland. At the end of the 1970s **Margaret Thatcher** swept to power and began a process of privatization and cuts in public services which was to leave few areas untouched.

In 1986, the stock market was deregulated (the 'Big Bang') but the boom which followed was short-lived, and the crash of the money markets in 1987 led to a deepening recession, which was exacerbated by a slump in property prices in 1988. In 1990, riots in Trafalgar Square against the **poll tax** signalled the beginning of the end for Margaret Thatcher, who was replaced as leader of the Conservative Party by John Major in October of that year. The seven years of growing dissatisfaction with Conservative rule that followed led to Tony Blair and his New Labour Party sweeping into power in May 1997.

Some grandiose new structures mark London's transition into the 21st century. Among them are the Millennium Dome in Greenwich, the conversion of Bankside Power Station into Tate Modern, and the innovative pedestrian Millennium Bridge linking Bankside with the city.

---

**SOCIAL UNREST**

During the Thatcher years social polarities in the capital increased, with stark contrasts between the huge increase in long-term unemployment and the conspicuous consumption enjoyed by the professional classes ('yuppies'). Riots erupted in Brixton in 1981 and Tottenham in 1985, and homelessness in the capital reached levels not witnessed since Victorian times. An area around the South Bank became known as 'Cardboard City' due to the number of vagrants living in cardboard shelters on the pavements. This has now been cleared out by the area's redevelopment, but dossers in London doorways remain a common site.

**Below:** *The controversial Millennium Dome at Greenwich, a multi-million-pound structure with an uncertain future.*

# GOVERNMENT AND ECONOMY

The UK is a constitutional monarchy, with the seat of government based in London. Britain has no written constitution and theoretically the Queen has the power to veto legislation, although her approval for new laws nowadays is more of a formality than anything else. The government of the day is led by the Prime Minister and his Cabinet of key ministers, who place legislation before Parliament for ratification. Sitting in the Palace of Westminster, Parliament consists of the 659 elected Members of the House of Commons and the unelected House of Lords. The latter came under fire as an anachronism (hereditary peers being able to overrule the elected Commons) and reform has begun by ousting some of the old peers. But this has been even more controversial because no replacement system has yet been decided.

## Local Government

In 1965, the London County Council was replaced by the **Greater London Council** (GLC), which controlled the entire 1580km$^2$ (610 sq miles) of Greater London and was responsible for a wide range of services and strategic planning. The GLC found itself at odds with central Government, a situation which reached its peak under the socialist GLC leader, 'Red Ken' Livingstone, in the 1980s. The GLC's introduction of subsidized public transport policies was anathema to the Thatcher government, who responded by abolishing the GLC in 1986. In May 1998, however, a referendum decided that Greater London should have an elected mayor and its own assembly, responsible for transport, fire, police and other services. Ironically the subsequent mayoral election (in 2000) put 'Red Ken' back in power.

## Economy

London continues to dominate in the political and financial arenas and leads the UK in many other areas including the arts, culture, fashion, publishing, retailing, the media and much else besides. Tourism is an important component of the service economy, with over 25 million annual visitors.

---

### GOVERNING LONDON

The first step towards the creation of a governing body – the mark of a true city – was the establishment of the Metropolitan Board of Works in 1855, which administered services such as street maintenance, sewage and lighting. In 1888, the London County Council (LCC) became the first elected ruling body and was responsible for building County Hall, its neoclassical headquarters (completed in 1920), opposite the Houses of Parliament. London now has 31 boroughs (plus the Cities of Westminster and London) and each has its own Lord Mayor (primarily a ceremonial post), of which the best known is the 'Lord Mayor of London' – actually the Lord Mayor of the City of London. The new post of 'Mayor of London', of which Ken Livingstone is the first incumbent, is an administrative job that covers the whole of the capital.

Although London is home to just 13% of the UK's population, it accounts for 16% of GDP (Gross Domestic Product); the GDP per capita is 30% higher than the national average.

Service industries make up the largest share of the metropolitan economy, with the concentration of financial, professional and business services reflecting the city's international role. But manufacturing still accounts for 11% of London's GDP. Pharmaceutical and medical research are also strong.

The capital is the UK's centre of higher education and among the world's centres for international finance, diplomacy, equity training, publishing, medical and scientific research, arbitration, media and creative industries.

London is the longest established of the world's three primary financial centres, and is the world's largest centre for foreign exchange trading, international bank lending, derivatives, reinsurance and Eurobonds. Eight of Europe's top 10 law firms are located in the city, reflecting the importance of London as a centre for international arbitration. As a centre for media and creative industries, it boasts a quarter of Europe's top 100 media companies.

London's standing as a global centre for international business is likely to be further enhanced as Britain integrates more fully into Europe.

**Above:** *The skyline of the City of London, a mosaic of modern architecture, is very impressive at night.*
**Below:** *The sumptuous interior of the stately House of Lords.*
**Opposite:** *The gilded statue of Justice sits atop the Old Bailey, or Central Criminal Court.*

**Above:** *The annual Notting Hill Carnival is the largest street festival in Europe.*

### LONDON'S POPULATION

**12th century** Beginnings of the capital: 18,000.
**14th century** Beginnings of overseas trade: 50,000.
**1348** Black Death wipes out half the population.
**16th century** Boom times under the Tudors: 200,000.
**1664–1665** Great Plague kills 70,000–100,000.
**1700** London is Europe's most populous city: 575,000.
**1801** First official census: One million.
**1900** Victorian expansion swells the city: 6–7 million.
**1939** Peak inter-war population: 8.7 million.
**1940–41** 30,000 killed in Blitz.
**1950s** Immigration from former colonies: 20,000 annual arrivals.
**1960s–70s** Decline of manufacturing and flight to the suburbs: 500,000 leave the capital.
**2000** Population: c.7 million.

## THE PEOPLE

For centuries London has been a cosmopolitan city, attracting people from other nations to live and work here. Refugees, traders, artists and others over the generations have flocked to what John Milton dubbed the 'mansion-house of liberty'. Today you will find not only the Irish (during the 19th century there were already over 100,000 Irish in London), Italians, Bangladeshis, Germans and West Indians but also Kurds, Somalis, Moroccans, Portuguese and people from every corner of the globe. One in five of London's 7 million residents belongs to a minority ethnic group and no less than 33 countries have resident communities of over 10,000 people who were born outside the UK and now live in the capital.

It is estimated that 200 languages are spoken in the city, and it is claimed that over 30% of Londoners are descended from first-, second- and third-generation immigrants. Writer HV Morton concluded in the 1940s that 'one of the charms of London is that there are no Londoners', while Evelyn Waugh bewailed the fact that 'The English are already hard to find in London. No-one lives there who is not paid to do so … I believe that London society has ceased to exist.'

### Ethnic London

London is by no means a homogenous entity and Londoners tend to associate more with the neighbour-hoods in which they live than with the city as a whole. There are no 'ghettos' as such, although immigrant groups have tended to settle in certain localities for particular reasons: Punjabi Sikhs, for instance, populated Southall in the vicinity of Heathrow Airport because it was near their point of arrival, and the airport offered work. Cypriots gravitated to Camden and Finsbury, where they could use their skills in the clothing trade, while Bengali Muslims moved to the area around Brick Lane in Tower Hamlets for similar reasons. The Chinese, too, moved into the East End – but, curiously, it was the introduction of public launderettes which largely put paid to their traditional laundry businesses and precipitated a switch to running Chinese restaurants in Soho. The Afro-Caribbean community has traditionally been based in Brixton, to the south of the river, and Notting Hill, west of the centre.

## London Neighbourhoods

While the 1960s witnessed some breaking down of the rigid class barriers of London society, Londoners still tend to be seen as haughty, snobbish and unfriendly by those who live in the provinces, and the smart districts – Mayfair, Knightsbridge, and Kensington – are still largely the preserve of the wealthy elite, while the East End is a steadfastly working class area. Meanwhile, from the 1970s onwards, the professional classes recolonized great swathes of North London – from Hampstead to Hackney – as well as areas south of the Thames (such as Camberwell and Greenwich) and property prices soared as gentrification led to a proliferation of wine bars, delicatessens and the like alongside the renovation of 19th-century terraces. During the 1980s the upwardly mobile 'yuppies' extended this process to Docklands, converting old warehouses into stylish 'loft apartments' and parking their Porsches in the shadow of long-defunct dockyard cranes.

Londoners tend to associate more with their locality or neighbourhood than might be imagined, venturing forth for shopping and entertainment to the West End or to the City and elsewhere to work. The City itself is a curious anomaly: formerly the heart of London, it has a resident population of only a little over 5000, but the daytime population soars to around half a million as the commuters arrive.

> ### COCKNEYS
>
> A 'Cockney' in the broadest sense is anyone born and bred in London, although it usually applies only to working class East End residents – traditionally, only those born within the sound of the bells of St Mary-le-Bow in Cheapside can claim to be true Cockneys. Cockney rhyming slang thrives in street markets and pubs: 'tit for tat' is a hat, 'apples and pears' are the stairs, and so on. Cockney 'Pearly Kings and Queens' put on their traditional, button-studded costumes for the Costermongers Pearly Harvest Festival Service held at the church of St Martin-in-the-Fields (Trafalgar Square) on the first Sunday in October every year. A 'costermonger' is someone who sells fruit and other produce from a market barrow, and this is essentially a harvest festival.

**Below:** *The 'Pearly Kings and Queens' in their traditional button-studded finery.*

## SPORTING VENUES

Tickets for major international
events can be extremely hard
to come by, and you need
to book well in advance
(sometimes several months).
● Crystal Palace National
Sports Centre,
tel: (020) 8778 0131;
● Lord's Cricket Ground,
tel: (020) 7289 1300;
● The Oval,
tel: (020) 7582 6660;
● Wembley Stadium,
tel: (020) 8902 0902;
● Ascot Racecourse,
tel: (01344) 622 211;
● Epsom Downs,
tel: (01372) 726 311;
● Kempton Park,
tel: (01932) 782 292;
● Sandown Park,
tel: (01372) 470 047;
● Windsor,
tel: (01753) 865 234;
● Twickenham Stadium,
tel: (020) 8831 6666;
● Wimbledon All England
Lawn Tennis Club,
tel: (020) 8946 2244.

It may be romanticizing the cohesion of local communities too much to claim that London is a collection of villages, but architecturally and otherwise the vestiges are still there in places such as Dulwich, Highgate, and Hampstead. While it may be the largest city in Europe, London is by no means a uniform entity as regards the people and the districts which comprise this great metropolis.

### Sport and Recreation

Whether you want to spectate or to become involved, there are numerous opportunities to participate in sporting activities in and around London. Many top international fixtures take place in the hallowed grounds of sporting venues such as **Lord's** (cricket), **Wimbledon** (tennis), **Crystal Palace** (athletics), **Wembley Stadium** (being redeveloped. Reopens 2004), and **Twickenham** (Rugby Union). In addition, world-famous horse races take place at locations such as **Ascot**, **Epsom**, and **Sandown Park**.

For those who want to do more than just watch, London offers opportunities for the sporty to take part in everything from aerobics to windsurfing. Council-run facilities provide inexpensive access to sports such as

tennis, swimming, weight-training, aerobics and so on. There are also numerous private gymnasiums and health clubs, including some in major hotels. London's parks, of course, offer opportunities for jogging, walking, tennis or boating.

**Athletics:** Major international events, as well as local contests, take place at the **Crystal Palace National Sports Centre**, with the two biggest competitions in early summer (June/July) and late summer (August).

**Cricket:** The cricket season runs from April to September. England's love of cricket is best appreciated on a sunny weekend afternoon, from a traditional pub overlooking the village green. Although dominated by arcane rules and peculiar terminology ('silly mid-offs', 'yorkers', 'googlies' and so on), the game can arouse fierce rivalry. The biggest drawcards of the season are the international **test matches** between England and touring teams, one of which is always played at **Lord's Cricket Ground** (the home of the Middlesex County Cricket Club) in St John's Wood, and another at **The Oval** in Kennington.

**Football:** Football (soccer) probably arouses more passion in the English than any other game, and although it is usually the big northern clubs which dominate the league tables, London prides itself on the strength of its teams such as Arsenal ('the Gunners'), Tottenham Hotspur (Spurs) and Chelsea. The season is from mid-August to early May, culminating in the FA Cup Final at Wembley Stadium.

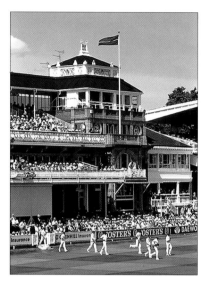

**Horse Racing:** A day at the races provides an entertaining insight into the personalities of the British people from all walks of life, with a flutter on the filly of your choice adding excitement to the occasion. Major race courses within easy reach of London include **Ascot** (with the highlight being the glamorous Royal Ascot meeting in June), **Epsom** (one of the world's fastest courses, home to Derby Day in June), **Kempton Park** (where meetings are far less snobby than elsewhere), **Sandown Park** (popular for day trips from the capital), and **Windsor** (which has a delightful setting alongside the Thames).

**Rugby:** There are two kinds of rugby (or rugger) played in Britain, **Rugby Union** (15-a-side) and **Rugby League** (13-a-side). In London there is one Rugby League team (the London Broncos), with other major teams (such as the Wasps, Harlequins and London Irish) playing Rugby Union. The season runs from September to April/May, culminating in the **Pilkington Cup** (the equivalent of the FA Cup Final), held at the end of April at the modern and impressive **Twickenham Stadium** in West London.

*Above: Lord's Cricket Ground, in St John's Wood, is one of London's most famous sporting venues.*

*Opposite: Around 30,000 people take part in the annual London Marathon.*

### LONDON MARATHON

Held in March/April, the Flora London Marathon follows a 40km (25 mile) course from Greenwich to Westminster and annually attracts around 30,000 participants. To participate, you must book before the end of September in the previous year. Details from the marathon hotline, tel: (09068) 334 450 (premium rate line).

**Right:** *Wimbledon is the setting for the prestigious lawn tennis championship: one of the sport's four Grand Slam events.*

**Tennis:** A climax of the international tennis season is the Grand Slam championship tournament, played on the famous grass courts at **Wimbledon** during the last week of June and the first week of July. Almost as famous for the cost of off-court strawberries as for the on-court antics of the international stars, tickets for the 'Wimbledon fortnight' are notoriously hard to obtain.

## The Arts

**Architecture:** The only vestiges of **Roman** Londinium are parts of the old Roman wall (visible at Tower Hill) and the ruins of the Temple of Mithras. **Norman** buildings are represented by the Tower of London and the church of St Bartholomew the Great in Smithfield, and the undercroft of Westminster Abbey. Most of the Abbey was rebuilt from the 13th century onwards in the **Medieval Gothic** style, other examples of which include Southwark Cathedral. The **Tudor** style tended to favour red brick over stone, with the most outstanding examples being Hampton Court Palace and St James's Palace.

The **English Renaissance** is best exemplified by the work of Inigo Jones, responsible for the Queen's House at Greenwich, the Banqueting House at Westminster, and the piazza in Covent Garden. The other great architect of the era was Sir Christopher Wren: following the Great Fire in 1666, Wren rebuilt St Paul's Cathedral and no less than 51 other churches in the City, as well as the

---

### HAPHAZARD PLANNING

London may have some of the finest architecture in the world but the city itself has developed over the centuries in a random fashion, with none of the great set pieces or rational planning of other major cities. The two focal points of its growth since medieval times are the City of London and Westminster, with development since the 18th century sprawling outwards to encompass a series of 'villages', which now form part of the huge conglomeration which is Greater London. One of the few set pieces of planning was John Nash's venture to create a fine boulevard (Regent Street) linking Piccadilly Circus (known as Regent Circus until 1880) with the former Marylebone Park, known as Regent's Park today.

Old Royal Observatory at Greenwich, the Royal Hospital in Chelsea, and numerous other landmarks. During the 18th century the neoclassical style was fashionable, when designer **Robert Adam** remodelled mansions such as Kenwood House, Osterley Park and Syon House. It was during this period that John Nash laid out Regent Street, linking St James's Palace with Regent's Park. The legacy of the **Georgian** period can be seen in the numerous elegant terraced houses which still exist in areas such as Bloomsbury, Islington, Greenwich, Dulwich and Hampstead.

During the **Victorian** era London was transformed by the building of new roads, railways, bridges, canals and docks. Prestigious buildings of this period (some harking back to the neoclassical or even Gothic traditions) include the British Museum, the Houses of Parliament, the National Gallery, Tower Bridge, the Natural History Museum and St Pancras Station. **Edwardian** London gave us the Old Bailey and department stores such as Whiteleys, Selfridges and Harrods. The city has few buildings from the **Modernist** era, and although there were once scores of Art Deco cinemas, most have now been demolished.

The **Postwar** period saw the building of the Royal Festival Hall, the unusual Common-wealth Institute, and dozens of concrete tower blocks (many of which are now being pulled down). Concrete also predominated in the construction of the South Bank Complex and the Barbican Centre complex.

Most **post-Modernist** architecture has been concentrated in the City and Docklands, notable structures including Lloyd's of London, the Canary Wharf tower, the Broadgate development next to Liverpool Street Station, the London Ark in Hammersmith, Waterloo International Terminal, the new British Library, the Channel 4 Television building, the Millennium Dome, the Millennium Bridge and the Tate Modern.

---

**THE GOSEE/WHITE CARD AND THE LONDON PASS**

The British Museum, the National Gallery and both Tates are free (apart from special exhibitions), but many other museums and galleries do charge, notably the superb group in South Kensington (*see* pp. 66–67). Keen gallery/museum goers can save money by purchasing a **GoSee card**. This covers 17 attractions, including the South Kensington museums, and is obtainable at any of them as well as tourist offices, transport terminals and some hotels. The card can be for 3 or 7 days, for an individual or the whole family. Another transport/attractions pass is the **London Pass**, website: www.londonpass.com

**Below:** *The 1931 Art Deco Broadcasting House, home of the BBC.*

### THEATRE TOURS

If you want to find out more about what goes on in some of London's famous theatres, you can take backstage tours (duration from 30 to 75 minutes) of several major theatres including the Royal National Theatre, South Bank Centre, tel: (020) 7452 3400 (tours), 7452 3000 (box office); and the Theatre Royal, Drury Lane, Catherine St, WC2, tel: (020) 7494 5000. Numbers are limited, so it's sensible to book in advance.

**Below:** *The Royal Academy, on Piccadilly, holds several exhibitions each year.*

**Art:** For the art lover, London offers not only some of the world's greatest collections of Western art but also a thriving contemporary scene with a huge range of new, creative talent on display. The historic collections that can be seen in the National Gallery, Tate, Courtauld Institute, British Museum and Victoria and Albert Museum will provide sufficient riches to sustain even the most ardent enthusiast.

In modern art, London has a number of dynamic young artists (names to watch out for include Damien Hirst, Helen Chadwick, Mat Collishaw, Fiona Rae and Anya Gallacio, amongst others) whose work can often be seen – for free – in the **commercial galleries** of Dering and Cork streets, both in the West End. The **Summer Exhibition** at the Royal Academy mostly features amateur artists, but the often controversial **Turner Prize** exhibits, which are displayed at Tate Britain in the month preceding the judging (November), are worth seeing. Another avenue to explore is the summer **degree shows** held at the various London art colleges in late May/June, in particular those at Goldsmiths, the Royal College, the Royal Academy, the Slade, and St Martin's School of Art.

**Theatre:** With a stage history that dates back to the father of theatre, William Shakespeare, it is little wonder that London is often considered the theatre capital of the world. While the West End may appear to be dominated by blockbusting musicals, numerous other stages provide the platform for inventive, talented work and original productions. London is home to two great acting companies, the **Royal Shakespeare Company** and the **Royal National Theatre**, but stars of the stage (and screen) can also be seen in numerous productions away from the West End or mainstream theatres. In addition, there is a thriving **fringe theatre** scene, with avant-garde plays staged in locations as diverse as pubs and converted warehouses.

In any one week there may be around 200 shows on the go, so you will be spoilt for choice.

**Classical Music, Opera and Dance:** London has a number of venues for classical music, ranging from the ornate splendour of the **Royal Albert Hall** to the three, purpose-built halls of the **South Bank Centre**, the acoustically

perfect **Wigmore Hall**, and the **Barbican Centre** complex, and on any one day there are likely to be several performances to choose from. The capital is home to the **Royal Philharmonic Orchestra**, the **London Symphony Orchestra**, the **London Philharmonic Orchestra**, the **Philharmonia**, and the **BBC Symphony Orchestra**, to name but the most prominent. Concerts are, in many cases, poorly attended (to the shame of Londoners), so there is rarely a problem getting tickets. You can take advantage of free **lunchtime concerts** from Monday to Friday in many churches (such as St Martin-in-the-Fields, St James's Church in Piccadilly, and several others). Outdoor concerts are also held at **Kenwood House** in the summer (*see* p. 89); a wide range of works is also performed during the **Henry Wood Promenade Concerts**, 'The Proms', (*see* p. 67) during the summer months.

Opera was first staged at the **Royal Opera House** in 1817, and performances still pack the house despite the exorbitant ticket prices. More reasonably priced performances can be seen at the **London Coliseum**, home to the **English National Opera**. New and innovative works are often performed during the summertime **Almeida Opera Festival** at the **Almeida Theatre** in Islington (*see* p. 90).

**Jazz** is also easy to find, notably at Ronnie Scott's Club (one night membership at the entrance). Booking advisable.

*Above: Popular theatre productions can run for decades. The Mousetrap is the longest running play in the world.*

---

**BRIGHT LIGHTS, BIG CITY**

The quality and variety of London's arts, culture and entertainment scene is probably unrivalled anywhere in the world. To navigate your way around this cultural maze, the most comprehensive listings of what's on are found in the weekly *Time Out*, and *What's On*, while the *Evening Standard* on Thursdays has an excellent listing supplement called *Hot Tickets*. Alternatively, call (premium rate):
• West End Shows, tel: (09068) 505 473;
• Productions beyond the West End, tel: (09068) 505 476;
• Rock and Pop Concerts, tel: (09068) 505 447;
• Current Exhibitions, tel: (09068) 505 441;
• What's on this week, tel: (09068) 505 440.

**Above:** *Tea at the Ritz is a British institution.*

Dance in all its varied forms is well represented in the capital, with every style from the classic showpieces of the **Royal Ballet** to contemporary works and even Brazilian or Indian dance on display. Major venues include the **ICA**, the **London Coliseum**, the **Royal Opera House**, **Riverside Studios** (Hammersmith), and the **South Bank Centre**. In addition, regional and international touring companies often perform in London. One of the best showcases for new talent is the annual **Dance Umbrella** festival, held in October/November.

## Food and Drink

British food may once have been something of an international joke, epitomized by things like comforting, stodgy pies and puddings ('nursery food'), greasy fish and chips, and mammoth fry-ups for breakfast. But that is an image which is well past its sell-by date, particularly in London, where the range of cuisines available is huge and the variety of eateries (from pubs to trendy cafés, brasseries, wine bars, bistros and the like) has expanded enormously in recent years. Coupled with this, there has been a revolution in top-end gourmet restaurants where home-grown talent is now proving itself to be a match for the best anywhere else in the world. Whatever your budget or taste buds dictate, you can be sure that London will provide plenty of culinary adventures.

The most characteristic British drinking venue is, of course, the 'public house' or **pub**, a social institution which stretches back to the days of wayside coaching inns. London has a vast diversity of pubs, many of them dating from the Victorian era, and there are very few

---

### AFTERNOON TEA

Afternoon tea is another great British institution which shouldn't be missed. Mostly the speciality of the grand hotels, the set tea usually involves 'finger' sandwiches (smoked salmon, cucumber and the like) followed by assorted cakes, scones with cream, or pastries, served with a selection of teas. Most of the big hotels have dress codes (no jeans or trainers) and in some (such as the Ritz) advanced bookings are required. Be prepared to dig deep: about £30 a head.

places where you won't find one within handy reach. Be warned though – they can be ghastly, with plastic decor, rude staff, terrible food and gassy beer (this is particularly true in the West End, where good pubs need some ferreting out). On the other hand, the best of them will feature a good range of 'real ales' (*see* p. 29), a welcoming atmosphere, tasty snacks and an entertaining ambience. Many are still the centre of the surrounding communities, with 'locals' propping up the bar and socializing. Many more have also been refurbished and feature fringe theatre or cabaret performances, live music, and even their own on-site micro-breweries. Good food, too, has become much more important in recent years, and lunchtime is the most popular time to eat in a pub (if possible try and avoid the 13:00–14:00 crush when they're packed out with office workers).

Wine is generally best avoided in pubs, and in this case you're better off heading for a **brasserie** or **wine bar**, of which there are scores throughout the capital. **Modern British Cuisine**: A new wave of restaurateurs and chefs have added spice and flair to British cuisine, proving that the capital is no longer the culinary backwater it was once thought to be – in fact, London now boasts more restaurants bearing the coveted Michelin star than any other European city apart from Paris.

'New wave' British cuisine includes chefs such as James Rix (at Alastair Little, Frith Street, Soho, W1), Matthew Harris (at Bibendum, Fulham Road, SW3), Jonathan Rickets (at St John, in St John St, EC1) and Mark Gregory (at Axis, Aldwych, WC2) who are all presently leading the way in top British cuisine. There is no overall style to this new wave, apart from a consistent sense of inventiveness and an eclectic use of

---

**TRADITIONAL BREAKFASTS**

Traditional British breakfasts are legendary, and are usually served up to around 11:00 in hotels and cafés (some serve them all day). The obligatory fry-up of eggs, bacon, sausage and tomato is often supplemented by extras such as 'bubble and squeak', chips, baked beans, mushrooms, black pudding, kedgeree or kidneys. After one of these hearty breakfasts you'll be well set up for a day's sightseeing.

**Below:** *The City Barge at Strand-on-the-Green, Chiswick: one of London's many pubs where you may enjoy a drink outside.*

## FISH AND CHIPS

Once considered to be the only worthwhile British culinary export to the world, fish and chips can be found almost everywhere – but standards vary widely. The best fish and chips are found in popular places such as the Sea Shell, (in Lisson Grove) and Geale's (at Notting Hill Gate). There are also many excellent seafood restaurants where you can enjoy Dover sole, plaice, sea bass, or even Cockney staples such as cockles, or eel pie and mash.

ingredients and methods which draws on everything from West Coast/Californian to Mediterranean and Far Eastern influences.

**Entertaining Themes:** Another recent phenomenon on the London restaurant scene has been the rise of mega entertainment and eating venues, pioneered by style guru Sir Terence Conran with the opening of the massive 350-seat Quaglino's restaurant in 1994; in 1995 he followed this with the even bigger (700-seat) Mezzo, which is on two floors with glass-fronted kitchens, comprising two restuarants, a café and three bars. Meanwhile, Marco Pierre White has continued to expand his empire, which now includes the Mirabelle, the Criterion Brasserie and Quo Vadis, which is decorated with artworks by Damien Hirst. Planet Hollywood (backed by Hollywood heavies Sylvester Stallone, Bruce Willis and Arnold Schwarzenegger) in Piccadilly and the Sports Café in the Haymarket are all part of the same trend, while the Rainforest Café (in Shaftsbury Avenue) has a jungle theme – with lots of vegetation, a tropical fish tank and animatronic elephants, gorilla and (in the shop) even a crocodile.

**Traditional British Food:** Alongside the growth of 'modern British' cuisine (*see* p. 27), there has also been a revival of traditional cooking in the capital's restaurants, with good, hearty food thankfully banishing the excesses of nouvelle cuisine to the culinary dustbin. Some restaurants, of course, never followed fashion anyway, and places such as the 150-year-old Simpson's in the Strand, and the Quality Chop House (EC1), have been serving staples such as steak and kidney pudding and fish cakes since time immemorial. Bangers and mash, meat casseroles and pies, shepherd's pie, toad-in-the-hole and

**Below:** *Simpson's in the Strand is a good place to sample traditional roast beef and Yorkshire pudding.*

**Left:** *Hand-pumped beer is just one of the hallmarks of a traditional London pub.*

roast beef with Yorkshire pudding are just some of the main courses you might come across. Desserts include treats such as jam roly-poly, sponges, trifles, toffee pudding, spotted dick and bread-and-butter pudding.

**Ethnic Restaurants:** London has always been known for its ethnic cuisine, in particular Indian, Bangladeshi and Chinese food. Many of the numerous curry houses tend to churn out identical dishes (with sauces bought in bulk) which have limited appeal, but to balance this there are many excellent establishments where freshly prepared ingredients are used to good effect in regional dishes from India, Nepal, Sri Lanka, Pakistan and Bangladesh. A similar caveat applies to Chinese restaurants, where monosodium glutamate (MSG) is heaped on regardless: however, London also has some of the best Cantonese chefs in Europe (partly due to an exodus from Hong Kong before it reverted to Chinese rule in 1997), with *dim sum* (lunchtime snacks) one of the most characteristic features of the cuisine.

The range of ethnic restaurants does not stop there, however, and among the ones you may come across are Japanese, Korean, Thai, Malaysian, Indonesian, Turkish, Jewish, Vietnamese, Mongolian and various types of African and Caribbean. French, Italian and Greek are probably the most widespread of the European cuisines, but virtually all the others are represented.

---

### REAL ALES

The classic British pub drink is a pint of **bitter**, a dark, uncarbonated brew that comes in many guises. The best bitters are those pumped by hand from the cellar, and served at room temperature. In previous decades the big breweries swallowed up many traditional small brewers and imposed a uniformly bland, gassy product on many pubs: thanks to the efforts of CAMRA (the Campaign for Real Ale) this trend was halted (if not reversed), and to taste the real thing you should avoid pubs where the beer is served by electric pump. Chilled, draught **lager** and bottled lagers are also widely available in pubs, as is Guinness, a dark, creamy Irish **stout.** The main London breweries are Youngs and Fullers.

# 2
# Whitehall and Westminster

**W**estminster, at the heart of the capital, has been the main seat of political and regal power for nearly a thousand years and consequently boasts some of London's most famous landmarks, such as the **Houses of Parliament**, **Big Ben** and **Westminster Abbey**. **Buckingham Palace** is nearby, as is **Trafalgar Square** with **Nelson's Column** and the **National Gallery**.

Westminster's role in the nation's history dates back to Edward the Confessor, who abandoned his predecessors' palace in the commercial heart of the city (2km/1¼ miles to the east) to build a grand church, 'West Minster', on a swampy site at the mouth of the River Tyburn, and a new palace alongside it so that he could supervise the project. The pious king died 10 days after his abbey was completed, but Westminster Palace remained as the monarch's main residence until it was damaged by fire, forcing Henry VIII to build a new one in Whitehall. The **Palace of Westminster** later became the Houses of Parliament, but Whitehall Palace burnt down in 1698, and the thoroughfare we now know as **Whitehall** – linking the Houses of Parliament with Trafalgar Square – became the preserve of government civil servants. Tony Blair's residence is located at **No. 11 Downing Street** on its west side.

All the area's main sights are within easy walking distance of each other, and there are connections to other parts of London along the river from Westminster Pier. Westminster itself is rather quiet – **Covent Garden** is the most lively area for food and entertainment.

## DON'T MISS

**\*\*\* Westminster Abbey:** with its hundreds of memorials embodying centuries of English history.
**\*\*\* Buckingham Palace:** Changing of the Guard. Visit the **State Rooms** in August–September.
**\*\*\* Tate Britain:** British art from the 16th century to the present.
**\*\*\* Trafalgar Square:** feed the pigeons and visit the **National Gallery**.
**\*\* Big Ben** and the **Houses of Parliament:** particularly attractive from the Thames.

**Opposite:** *The Houses of Parliament, 'birthplace of democracy'.*

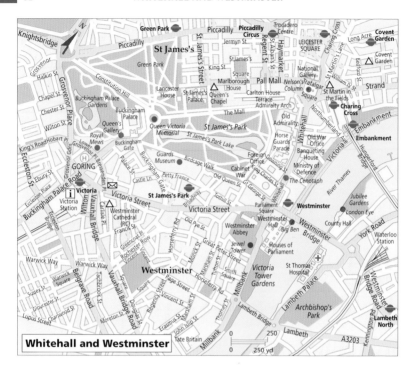

**Whitehall and Westminster**

## ALONG WHITEHALL

This broad, 1km-long avenue links Trafalgar Square with Parliament Square, and is lined with buildings housing key government offices and ministries. It was named after the former Whitehall Palace, where Henry VIII lived for his last 14 years. The palace was destroyed by fire in 1698, and only the **Banqueting House** (open 10:00–16:30, Monday–Saturday), which was built by Inigo Jones for James I, remains. The wonderful ceiling in the main dining hall was painted by Rubens. He was commissioned by Charles I, who was put to death outside this hall in 1649. Stepping through the window on to the scaffolding outside, he wore several shirts in case he should shiver from the cold and the crowd mistake this for fear. After the execution, his head was sewn back on before the corpse was taken for burial at Windsor.

## Horse Guards *

Opposite the Banqueting House is the **Horse Guards**, once the old palace guard house, where the impassive troopers of the Queen's Household Cavalry stand outside their sentry boxes or on horseback. During the celebrated Changing of the Guard (*see* p. 32), mounted troopers in full livery ride up from Hyde Park Barracks via Hyde Park Corner, to the **Horse Guards Parade** on the other side of the building where the ceremony takes place.

## Downing Street

Past the Old Treasury on the same side of Whitehall as the **Horse Guards** is the home of the British Prime Minister. No. 10 was presented to Britain's first Prime Minister, Sir Robert Walpole, in 1732, and remained the PM's residence until Tony Blair decided it was too small and took over No. 11, traditionally home of the Chancellor of the Exchequer.

**Above:** *The Old Admiralty faces on to the Horse Guards, the setting for the Trooping of the Colour.*
**Below:** *Colourful pageantry provides a free spectacle for visitors to the city.*

## The Cenotaph *

Erected in 1919 to commemorate those whose lives were lost during World War I, the Cenotaph is the main focus of the Remembrance Sunday ceremony, which is held every November. A two-minute silence is observed for those who died in both World Wars.

## Cabinet War Rooms **

Just down King Charles Street off Whitehall's west side are the **Cabinet War Rooms**, the underground headquarters of Churchill, the War Cabinet and Chiefs of Staff during World War II bombing raids. They include Churchill's bedroom, study and the Map Room. Open 09:30–17:15 daily, April–Sept; 10:00–17:15, Oct–March.

### PARLIAMENT SQUARE

Laid out soon after the rebuilding of the Houses of Parliament in the mid 1800s, Parliament Square is a rather busy traffic roundabout and houses some of London's most famous landmarks, such as the Houses of Parliament, Big Ben and Westminster Abbey. There are several interesting statues dotted about Parliament Square, including those of Abraham Lincoln, Jan Smuts and a glowering Winston Churchill (in the southeast corner of the green).

### Houses of Parliament ★★★

The 'Mother of all Parliaments' is one of London's best-known sights, a grandiose Victorian edifice on the north bank of the Thames which has been the site of parliamentary meetings since 1265. The 266m (872ft) riverside façade is best appreciated from Westminster Bridge, or the south bank of the Thames, with the imposing Victoria Tower to the west and the clock-tower, containing the bell known as Big Ben, to the east.

The House is divided into upper and lower houses, the **House of Commons** and the **House of Lords**. A wartime bomb destroyed the original Commons debating chamber, and reconstruction was completed in 1950. On the other side of the Central Lobby is the House of Lords, a far more splendid chamber where debates are usually less acrimonious.

---

**INSIDE PARLIAMENT**

If Parliament is in session at night, a light is lit at the top of Big Ben. Debates in the House of Commons take place Mon–Wed 14:30–22:30 and Thurs 11:30–19:00, but there are variations. Visitors can watch from the Strangers Gallery by queuing at St Stephen's Gate on Parliament Square: it can take over an hour to get in. Advance tickets are needed for Prime Minister's Question Time, Wed 15:00: contact your local MP or embassy/high commission. Notes on the more arcane proceedings of the Commons are supplied. Parliament is in recess during summer (August to mid-October), and at Christmas and Easter.

---

**Above:** *The clock-tower commonly called 'Big Ben'.*
**Right:** *The Houses of Parliament are an impressive sight from across the Thames, and the London Eye provides an unusual view.*

Facing Parliament Square on the north side of the House is **Westminster Hall**, the only surviving relic of the original palace. Across the road from the Houses of Parliament is the 14th-century **Jewel Tower,** which now houses an exhibition on parliament's history. Open daily 10:00–17:30.

### Westminster Abbey ***

A masterpiece in its own right, the Abbey also presents a rich pageant of English history and has been the setting for almost every Coronation since 1066.

Built on the site of a monastery in the 11th century, the present church mostly dates from the 13th century and its soaring, 30m (98ft) nave is the loftiest in the country.

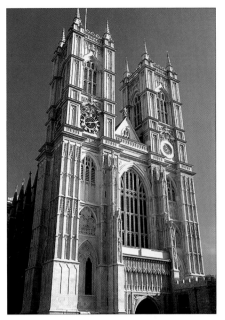

It would take a whole book to describe the hundreds of memorials which fill the Abbey, but the highlights include the Tomb of the Unknown Warrior (representing British troops who died in World War I), the Perpendicular Henry VII Chapel, the Coronation Chair, the Royal Chapels, Statesman's Corner and Poet's Corner.

**Above:** *Westminster Abbey contains the tombs of many medieval monarchs.*

### Tate Britain ***

Heading west from Parliament Square, you reach Millbank, home of what was the Tate Gallery and is now Tate Britain, the non-British works having been transferred to **Tate Modern**. Both galleries will continue to have innovative and controversial exhibitions of contemporary works. Tate Britain still houses the renowned Turner collection (some 282 paintings and 20,000 drawings, though not all on display simultaneously), and is where works competing for the Turner prize are displayed. Other old British favourites are also exhibited.

---

**EXPLORING THE ABBEY**

There is a charge to visit the Abbey (entrance via the north transept, expect queues in summer). Open 09:30–16:45 Mon–Fri, 09:30–14:45 Sat. Audio guides are available, and guided tours are offered by the Abbey's vergers. For details and bookings, tel: (020) 7222 7110. There is a separate charge to visit the Chapter House and Museum, open ±10:00–16:00 daily – according to natural light.

**Above:** *Buckingham Palace is a 'must' on every tourist itinerary.*
**Opposite:** *St James's Park is one of the great London parks, where you can relax on a deckchair listening to the band, feed the ducks or take a leisurely stroll.*

---

### NASH AND THE PALACE

Buckingham House, which originally stood on this site, was the home of the Duke of Buckingham until 1762 when it was sold to George III. His successor, George IV, commissioned his favourite architect (John Nash) to expand and overhaul the house, but it wasn't until the 19-year-old Queen Victoria acceded to the throne in 1837 that it became the official Royal Palace. Nash had placed a triumphal arch in front of the palace but in 1851 this was moved to its present site in Hyde Park and is now called the Marble Arch.

---

## ROYAL LONDON

### Buckingham Palace ★★★

The official London residence of the monarch since Queen Victoria's reign, Buckingham Palace is a vast monolith which impresses by virtue of its size rather than by any architectural graces it may possess.

Apart from those select few who are invited to the Queen's summer garden parties, the Palace has only been open to the public since 1993, when it was decided to admit visitors to help defray the costs of rebuilding Windsor Castle after a disastrous fire (*see* pp. 112–113). The Palace is only accessible during August and September (open 09:30–16:30 daily) when the Queen and her family are at their summer retreat in Balmoral.

The tickets are timed but, once in, linger to examine the works of art in 19 of the 600 rooms in the Palace, the most impressive being the richly decorated Throne Room, the State Dining Room, the Blue Drawing Room and the Music Room. The Ballroom is the setting for investitures and entertainment, while the White Drawing Room is where the family gathers. The Queen's Gallery has closed for extensive renovation and will not reopen until 2002.

Further down Buckingham Palace Road, visit the working stables of the **Royal Mews** (open 12:00–15:30, Mon–Thurs, Oct–July; 10:30–16:00 Mon–Thurs, Aug–Sept). The original Kings Mews were pulled down to make way for Trafalgar Square, and both the new mews and Trafalgar Square were designed by **John Nash**, who was commis-

sioned by the Prince Regent (later crowned George IV).
The main attractions of the mews are the magnificent
gilded and polished state carriages and coaches, which
have been used for every Royal Coronation since 1831.

## The Mall *

This broad, tree-lined boulevard sweeps down from the
**Victoria Memorial** outside Buckingham Palace to the
enormous **Admiralty Arch**, which frames the southwest
corner of Trafalgar Square.

South of the Mall is **St James's Park**, Henry VIII's
hunting reserve first opened to the public by Charles II,
who liked to walk here with his mistress. The attractive
lake in the park is home to ducks and Canada geese.

On the north side of the Mall at the Buckingham Palace
end are **Lancaster House** and **Clarence House** (neither is
open to public viewing; the latter is the home of the
Queen Mother). A little further east lies **St James's Palace**,
which was the sovereign's residence prior to the reconstruction of Buckingham Palace, and which now provides
a London home for the Prince of Wales.

The **Chapel Royal**, St James's Palace, can be viewed
during Sunday services (8:30 and 11:15, Oct–Good Friday),
as can the **Queen's Chapel**, Marlborough Road (8:30 and
11:15, Easter Sun–end July). Both are closed Aug–Sept.

Past **Marlborough House** (designed by Wren) is the
impressive façade of Carlton House Terrace, built by
John Nash under the patronage of George IV.

From the **Duke of York's
Steps** in the middle of the terrace
there are views across St James's
Park, and to the east of the steps
is the entrance to the **Institute of
Contemporary Art,** or ICA, a
trendy hangout for London's
avant-garde set. The ICA has a
regular and varied programme of
films, talks, exhibitions and other
events. The ICA Art Gallery is
open 12:00–19:30, daily.

> ### THE CHANGING OF THE GUARD AT BUCKINGHAM PALACE
>
> This free spectacle on the
> forecourt of **Buckingham
> Palace** still draws in the
> crowds as it has done for
> decades. The New Guard
> marches down from
> **Wellington Barracks** to
> arrive at the Palace just after
> 11:30, and the band plays
> while the keys are ceremo-
> nially handed over. The Old
> Guard then returns to the
> barracks, leaving the Palace
> in the hands of the New
> Guard until the following
> morning. The ceremony takes
> place daily from May–August,
> alternate days September–
> April; it may be cancelled in
> wet weather.

**Below:** *Nelson gazes out from the top of his column in Trafalgar Square.*

## TRAFALGAR SQUARE

The largest non-park public area in London, Trafalgar Square formed part of architect John Nash's grand designs to transform the city in the mid-19th century. The square was named after Nelson's famous naval victory over the French in 1805, and the 52m (170ft) **Nelson's Column** – the focal point of the square – was finished in 1843, as was the National Gallery on its north side. The famous lions at the base of the column were added in 1867, but the fountains were not installed until 1936, nearly 70 years later.

On the west side of the square is the neoclassical Canada House (originally the Royal College of Physicians), whose Portland Stone façade is echoed on the east side by South Africa House. The best view over Trafalgar Square is from the steps of the National Gallery, looking down past Nelson's Column and along the length of Whitehall to Big Ben beyond.

Tucked into the northeast corner of the square is **St Martin-in-the-Fields**, built in 1726. It has a fine Corinthian portico, topped by an unusual tower and steeple, and the interior boasts an Italian plasterwork ceiling. There's a small craft and clothes market outside the church, and the crypt houses a brass-rubbing centre.

In December the square is lit up by an enormous, beautifully decorated Christmas tree. A tree is donated annually by Norway in thanks to Britain for its role in the country's liberation from the Nazis during World War II.

## The National Gallery ***

Housing one of the world's greatest permanent art collections, the National Gallery contains over 2000 paintings, including famous works of the Old Masters. The collection was begun as late as 1824 with only a few pieces, but today the scope – spanning Western Art from 1260 to 1900 – is so enormous that it is impossible to absorb it all in one go. If you are pressed for time, the *20 Great Paintings* booklet (obtainable at the Gallery) will prove helpful. The gallery was given a new lease of life with the opening of the five-storey Sainsbury Wing (funded by the supermarket chain) in 1991, which houses the Early Renaissance Collection. If you want to peruse the paintings chronologically, the Sainsbury Wing is the place to start. Open 10:00–18:00, Thursday–Tuesday; 10:00–21:00, Wednesday.

## The National Portrait Gallery **

Founded in 1856, the National Portrait Gallery houses some 10,000 portraits (including paintings, drawings, sculptures and photographs) of famous men and women from the Middle Ages to the present day. From politicians to poets, and from royalty to pop stars, there is something for everyone to enjoy in this entertaining collection. It starts with the Tudors on the top floor, working down to post-war personalities on ground floor level. The Gallery houses the only known portrait of William Shakespeare. Open 10:00–18:00, Monday–Wednesday, Saturday, Sunday; 10:00–21:00, Thursday and Friday.

### THE NATIONAL GALLERY

The majority of the capital's modern and British collections of art are found in **Tate Modern** and **Tate Britain**, while the main strengths of the **National Gallery** are in early Renaissance Italian, Dutch, and 17th-century Spanish paintings. Some of the star attractions include the **Leonardo Cartoon** (chalk drawing of the Virgin and Child with St John the Baptist, 1510); the **Baptism of Christ** by Piero della Francesca (a pioneer of early Renaissance perspective, 1450); the **Rokeby Venus** by Diego Velázquez (1649); John Constable's **Haywain** (classic portrayal of the English countryside, 1821) and Hans Holbein's **The Ambassadors** (1533).

**Opposite above:**
*The National Gallery and St Martin-in-the-Fields on the north side of Trafalgar Square.*
**Left:** *Trafalgar Square at Christmas. The giant Christmas tree is an annual gift from Norway.*

# 3
# The West End

Although it is situated in the heart of the city, the West End acquired its name during the 19th century, when this area, west of the original commercial centre, became a desirable residential district, and smart shops and upmarket hotels established themselves among the city's formal squares and mews terraces. Today the West End is the capital's principal shopping and entertainment district.

London's major theatres and cinemas are concentrated around **Leicester Square** and **Piccadilly Circus**, which form part of **Soho**. Traditionally, Soho has been home to immigrants from Irish, Israeli, Italian, Chinese and even Huguenot descent. The invention of the laundromat forced the Chinese to diversify from traditional laundry businesses in the East End to restaurant ownership. **Chinatown** is now one of the best-known areas in which to enjoy a cheap, tasty meal after the theatre or cinema.

Soho's Bohemian atmosphere has always attracted writers, artists and musicians, and, more recently, media folk. Its dual personality is evident in the existence of porn shops alongside smart clubs and trendy shops. It was largely to distance the up-and-coming area around Mayfair from the relative squalor of Soho that **Regent Street** was laid out in the early 1800s, when over 700 houses and small shops were demolished to make way for Nash's grand design. Today Regent Street and **Bond Street**, are among the capital's classiest shopping streets. Nearby **Savile Row** is famed as the home of bespoke English tailoring. **Oxford Street**, to the north, provides a vast range of shops along its busy length.

## DON'T MISS

\*\*\* **Soho:** soak up the bohemian atmosphere.
\*\***BBC Experience:** take part in a recording and learn about broadcasting
\*\* **Piccadilly:** English tea at the **Ritz** or **Fortnum's**.
\*\* **Charing Cross Road:** browse the bookshops, see the **Photographer's Gallery**.
\*\* **Piccadilly Circus:** see it by night, followed by a show at a West End theatre.
\*\* **Bond Street** and **Regent Street:** window-shopping in the exclusive stores.
\* **Chinatown:** exotic super-markets and great food.

**Opposite:** *Regent Street curves to the north from busy Piccadilly Circus.*

## Soho

One of the city's most colourful areas, Soho buzzes with activity 24 hours a day, particularly by night. Once London's principal red-light district, it has been cleaned up in recent years (although strip joints, including the famous Raymond Revuebar, still operate) and now offers a vast range of fashionable cafés, brasseries, restaurants, discos, clubs and, of course, cinemas and theatres.

**Shaftesbury Avenue** is one of the main theatre areas, and also has a few cinemas and clubs (such as the Limelight Club). Parallel to Shaftesbury Avenue, **Old Compton Street** is typical of the peculiar mixture which characterizes Soho, with sex shops rubbing shoulders with Continental patisseries and cafés, fashion boutiques, gay bars, trendy brasseries and specialized food shops.

There are many interesting little nooks and crannies to be discovered while wandering around the network of streets in this vicinity. **Frith Street** has a plaque on the house where Mozart once stayed, and it was in a room above a restaurant here that John Logie Baird gave the first ever public demonstration of his new invention, the television, in 1926. Ronnie Scott's famous jazz club was founded here in 1958. **Dean Street** boasts a plaque to Karl Marx. Soho's vice rackets are mostly concentrated to the west of **Wardour Street**, where you will also find **Berwick Street Market** (a good place to buy fruit), which runs into the Rupert Street market (mainly clothes and jewellery), both of which operate Monday–Saturday.

### Charing Cross Road *

Dividing Soho from Covent Garden to the east, Charing Cross Road boasts several theatres and the highest concentration of bookshops in the city. Other than the

---

### HALF-PRICE THEATRE

On the south side of Leicester Square, the Society of West End Theatres operates a **ticket booth** where you can get seats for the day's performance at half-price +£2 for most West End shows. The booth opens daily at 12:00, closing at 15:00 on Sunday, 18:30 on other days. Tickets are never available for sell-out shows, but can sometimes be bought in advance from official booking agencies such as First Call, tel: (020) 7420 0000, or Ticketmaster, tel: (020) 7344 4444, if you are prepared to pay hefty booking fees. Buying from touts outside theatres is not advisable.

rambling expanses of Foyle's and Waterstone's there
are numerous specialist and second-hand bookshops,
particularly in **Cecil Court** below Leicester Square tube
station. Nearby is the excellent **Photographer's Gallery**
which has interesting (and free) exhibitions. Open
11:00–18:00, Monday–Saturday; 12:00–18:00 on Sunday.

## Leicester Square *

Adjoining Charing Cross Road, Leicester Square is where
all the big movies are premiered and it also has several
popular clubs and discos at its fringes. The garden at the
centre of the square features a statue of Charlie Chaplin,
while a wide variety of street performers make the north
side their stage, as do street artists who are happy to
create souvenir portraits.

## Chinatown *

To the north of Leicester Square is Chinatown, a small
enclave focused around Gerrard Street with its red-and-
gold gateways and pagoda-style telephone boxes.
Chinese supermarkets and ornament shops co-exist
alongside numerous restaurants, open late into the
night, where you can find everything from Cantonese
cuisine to crispy duck. The restaurants here (particularly
the smaller ones which look more like cafés) are usually
reasonably priced, and full to overflowing on Sundays
with Chinese families tucking into their *dim sum*.

---

**CHINESE NEW YEAR**

If you're in the city for
the **Chinese New Year**
(late Jan or early Feb) head
down to **Gerrard Street** to
witness one of the noisiest
celebrations in the capital,
with firecrackers exploding
everywhere as colourful
papier-mâché lions dance
through Chinatown trying
to grab the cabbages, decorated with bank notes, which
residents hang from their
windows. This exuberant
event attracts Chinese
people, as well as sight-
seers, from all over London.

**Opposite:** *London's
famous 'black' cabs in
Shaftesbury Avenue, where
several theatres are located.*
**Left:** *Chinese New
Year is a colourful and
joyous celebration when
Chinatown comes alive
with dragons and parades.*

## PICCADILLY AND REGENT STREET
### Piccadilly Circus *

Originally known as Regent Circus and forming part of Nash's grand plan for Regent Street, Piccadilly Circus is one of the main hubs of the West End and a popular tourist spot – although Londoners are more likely to curse the traffic or pedestrian congestion and wonder what on earth everybody is doing here.

### Trocadero **

One of the main attractions of Piccadilly Circus, apart from the statue of **Eros**, is the three-storey Trocadero complex, with its fascinating shops and several hi-tech interactive entertainment centres featuring the latest in electronic wizardry.

Piccadilly is no stranger to outlandish entertainment: in the 1830s the **Egyptian Hall** displayed Siamese twins, the 2ft-high 'General' Tom Thumb, and a mermaid (half-monkey, half-fish), among other curiosities. The modern equivalent is the **Trocadero Centre**, a shopping, eating and entertainment complex which includes a multi-screen cinema, the 40-metre **Troc Drop** (the world's first indoor free-fall ride) and **Funland**, home to an ever-increasing, ever-changing assortment of hi-tech interactive games and rides, as well as such old favourites as dodgems and bowling alleys. The centre is open 10:00–midnight daily, and until 01:00 on Friday and Saturday evenings. Neighbours include the **Planet Hollywood** restaurant and **Rock Circus**, where animatronic waxworks mime in co-ordination with individual headphones as you travel the historical road of rock'n'roll, so you can enjoy the sort of music you like and skip through what you don't. Open 10:00–21:00 Friday, Saturday, 11:00–20:00 Tuesday, 10:00–20:00 Sunday, Monday, Wednesday and Thursday.

**Below:** *Piccadilly Circus, lit by vast neon hoardings.*

## Regent Street **

The section of Regent Street that curves between Oxford Circus and Piccadilly Circus is a prime shopping zone, featuring such renowned stores as Hamleys, Aquascutum and Liberty. At the southern end is the **Café Royal**, once frequented by such luminaries as Oscar Wilde and George Bernard Shaw and retaining an air of faded grandeur.

Behind Hamleys, to the east, is **Carnaby Street**, a focal point of the 'Swinging Sixties' and now a cheap shopping area.

North of Oxford Circus is Portland Place, home of **Broadcasting House**. Round the back is the entrance to the **BBC Experience**; behind-the-scenes tours take you through broadcasting history, allowing you to participate in a recording, before exploring an interactive zone covering many aspects of radio and TV broadcasting.

*Above: The Tudor-style façade of Liberty, one of London's most exclusive department stores, famous for its fabric designs.*
*Below: The luxurious Fortnum & Mason where you may, among other things, purchase many varieties of tea and other traditional English fare in the ground-floor food hall.*

## Piccadilly **

Leading from Piccadilly Circus down to Hyde Park Corner, **Piccadilly** is a busy road where you can take afternoon tea at famous establishments such as the **Ritz Hotel** or **Fortnum & Mason**, the epicurean emporium which supplies delicacies to the Royal household, and magnificent picnic hampers for society events.

Behind Fortnum & Mason, there is a small enclave between Piccadilly and the Mall, which has been a fashionable haunt since Henry VIII built St James's Palace in the 1530s, with courtiers and pillars of society disporting themselves ever since in its smart shops and exclusive clubs.

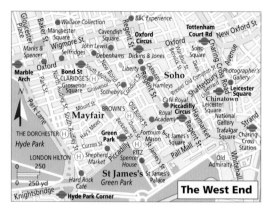

The West End

At the heart of this exclusive area is **St James's Square**, laid out in the 1670s. Some houses here have seen a succession of illustrious residents: No. 10 was home to prime ministers Pitt the Elder, Lord Derby and Gladstone (today it houses the offices of the prestigious Royal Institute for International Affairs). No. 4 was the home of Nancy Astor, who became the first female MP to sit in the House of Commons in 1919. During World War II, both General Eisenhower and General de Gaulle had headquarters here. At No. 14 is the **London Library**, a private lending library founded by historian Thomas Carlyle.

To the west of St James's Square can be found the auctioneers, **Christie's**, while just to the south is the unusual **Schomberg House**, with a 17th-century red brick façade; the painter, Gainsborough, lived here in the last years of his life.

Located to the north of St James's Square and running parallel with Piccadilly is **Jermyn Street**, one of London's most elegant shopping streets. Among the windows that are worth peering into along here are those of Davidoff (cigars), Turnbull & Asser (shirts), Floris (perfumes), and Bates (hatters). On the corner where Jermyn Street meets Duke Street is the famous Dunhill shop, which houses a small museum, open during shop hours Monday–Saturday, and covering mainly smoking-related objects.

In St James's Place is **Spencer House**, a splendid 18th century town house built for the first Earl of Spencer, ancestor of the late Diana, Princess of Wales. In the 1980s Lord Rothschild restored it to its original magnificence, and guided tours are available 10:30–16:45 on Sundays (closed January and August).

**Opposite:** *The Burlington Arcade, built in the 19th century, houses many small and exclusive shops.* **Below:** *Floris in Jermyn Street, purveyors of fine fragrances since 1730.*

On Piccadilly itself is **St James's Church**, built by Wren in 1684 and said to have been his favourite amongst the many London churches he was responsible for. Although much altered since then (partly due to bomb damage in 1940), it still features an airy, graceful interior and an ornate altar screen carved by the 17th-century master Grinling Gibbons; the organ was moved here from the chapel at the Whitehall Palace in 1691. William Blake and Pitt the Elder were baptised in this church, which today hosts society weddings, lectures, and concerts, as well as ministering to the homeless and hosting markets: antiques on Tuesday, arts and crafts Wednesday–Saturday.

## Gentlemen's Clubs *

Pall Mall and St James's Street are famous for their private clubs, many of which still traditionally exclude women. Most were founded in the early 19th century. The oldest is **White's** (with a membership which includes Prince Charles, top politicians, and military brass), while the **Carlton Club** is favoured by top Tories and the **Reform Club** was traditionally the home of the Liberals.

## The Burlington Arcade **

On the other side of Piccadilly is the superb Regency Mall, the Burlington Arcade, with delightful mahogany-fronted shops selling smart shirts, luggage, jewellery and other pricey items. Next door, Burlington House is home to the **Royal Academy**. Founded in 1768, it holds many exhibitions annually, including the well-known Summer Exhibition, and is reached via a paved piazza designed specifically for changing exhibitions of sculptures. Open 10:00–18:00, Saturday–Thursday; 10:00–20:30 Friday. The ethnographic collections which temporarily formed the **Museum of Mankind** in Burlington Street have now returned to the British Museum (*see* p. 53). Almost opposite is **Savile Row**, the home of some of Britain's most exclusive tailors.

| CHRISTMAS LIGHTS |
| --- |

During the pre-Christmas rush there is no busier place than Oxford Street and the surrounding area, with traffic wardens continually marshalling shoppers to stop them from blocking the roads or falling under the wheels of a bus. Most are probably busy gawking at the famous **Christmas lights** which adorn the streets from November onwards. Oxford Street, Regent Street and Bond Street usually all have **lighting up ceremonies** where celebrities throw the switches, and various jollities are provided, including carol singers, horse-drawn carriages, choirs, musicians, seasonal refreshments and, of course, late-night shopping. Contact the Tourist Board (*see* Tourist Information, p. 122) for exact dates.

*Above: Shepherd Market is a popular spot for al fresco eating during the summer.*

### A DAY AT SELFRIDGES

One of the great landmarks of Oxford Street is the imposing, colonnaded façade of **Selfridges**, which opened in 1909, just four years after Harrods in Knightsbridge, and challenged the latter's dominance by marketing itself as being 'dedicated to the service of women'. 'Why not spend a day at Selfridges?' was the novel theme promoted by its owner, Chicago millionnaire Gordon Selfridge. One of its original Art Deco lifts is now in the Museum of London (*see* p. 74). In 1927, Selfridge purchased Whiteleys in Queensway, which had gone into decline after its founder William Whiteley (a role model for Selfridge) had been murdered. It was Whiteley who had claimed to supply everything 'from a pin to an elephant' – a slogan that was later associated with Harrods.

## MAYFAIR AND OXFORD STREET
### Mayfair *

Situated to the north of Piccadilly, Mayfair is one of the most upmarket residential areas in London. It is an aristocratic enclave where major landowners such as the Berkeleys and Grosvenors built grand squares (which still bear their names) surrounded by palatial mansions in the middle of the 18th century. Embassies, consulates and swish hotels (such as Claridges) now predominate, with some of the city's top shopping districts, clubs and casinos (in St James's and Curzon Street respectively) within convenient reach.

Mayfair is bordered on the west by **Park Lane**, where luxury hotels such as the Dorchester, Grosvenor and Hilton enjoy views over Hyde Park.

### Shepherd Market *

Between Mayfair and Piccadilly lies a maze of alleys and passageways, which still retain a village-like atmosphere. Here you will find a number of fashionable restaurants and pubs, from which people overflow onto the pavements in summer.

### Bond Street **

Cutting right through the heart of Mayfair, Bond Street (divided into New Bond Street in the north and Old Bond Street in the south) harbours some of the most

exclusive and expensive shops in London: Chanel, Asprey & Garrard, Cartier, Versace and Hermès are all found along here. Bond Street is also noted for its fine art galleries, and its resident auctioneers, Sotheby's.

**Left:** *The Hard Rock Café is one of London's most popular eating places and something of an institution.*
**Below:** *Two of London's most famous shops have combined to become Asprey & Garrard, on Bond Street – a luxurious choice if you are shopping for jewellery, silver, china or other exclusive gift items.*

### Oxford Street *

One of London's best-known shopping areas, Oxford Street was developed as long ago as the 1780s to cater for the wealthy residents who were at that time moving out of the old city centre into more fashionable areas in the West End. This 2km (1 mile) street is still one of the world's most profitable retailing districts despite numerous recessions and very high rents. There are also a number of good quality department stores such as Marks & Spencer, Selfridges, John Lewis and Debenhams.

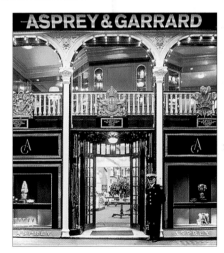

Off Oxford Street to the north of Manchester Square is the **Wallace Collection** in Hertford House (open 10:00–17:00, Monday–Saturday; 14:00–17:00, Sunday), which offers a fabulous display of European art (particularly 18th century works), and an impressive armoury.

# 4
# Bloomsbury and Covent Garden

A stone's throw from the busy shops of Oxford Street and adjacent Tottenham Court Road (the main centre for hi-fi and computer retailing in London), **Bloomsbury** is, by contrast, a low-key area known for its many pleasant public squares and literary associations. Home to London University, University College Hospital and numerous book publishers, the area was also the birthplace of the famous Bloomsbury Group during the inter-war years, an intellectual circle of friends that included Virginia Woolf, DH Lawrence, Bertrand Russell, EM Forster and Lytton Strachey. Today the main attraction in the area is the **British Museum**, a venerable institution which is undergoing a major transformation: London's first covered square – and one of its most imaginative public spaces – is being created at the heart of this historic museum.

To the south of Bloomsbury, High Holborn leads to the tranquil legal enclaves of the historical buildings of the **Inns of Court**, the main centre of jurisprudence in the city for the last 700 years.

One of the liveliest areas of central London, **Covent Garden** was once the capital's main market for fruit, flowers and vegetables until the wholesale market was moved out to a purpose-built complex south of the Thames near Battersea in 1974. In the last two decades it has been redeveloped and has gradually blossomed as a tourist attraction in its own right, bursting with trendy wine bars and restaurants, smart clothes shops, arts and crafts markets and almost non-stop street entertainment.

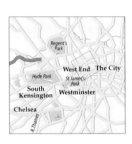

### DON'T MISS

**\*\*\* British Museum:** outstanding collections. Follow up with a stroll around Bloomsbury's leafy squares and a visit to **Dickens' House**.
**\*\*\* Gilbert Collection:** stunning decorative arts.
**\*\*\* Covent Garden:** markets, shops and restaurants of this trendy area.
**\*\* The Courtauld:** Impressionist and Post-Impressionist collections.
**\*\* Sir John Soane's Museum:** eclectic collections in Holborn.

**Opposite:** *Covent Garden's market hall, built in the 1830s, was London's produce market for over 100 years.*

## BLOOMSBURY

This area has a pleasant architectural coherence, and its leafy, Georgian squares (among them **Russell Square**, **Bedford Square**, **Gordon Square**, and **Tavistock Square**) provide a tranquil respite from the hubbub of city life in London. On the eastern fringes of Bloomsbury is **Dickens' House** which is in fact only one of 15 houses that the novelist occupied in London. The interior boasts letters, pictures, manuscripts, and original furniture from Dickens' time, giving an interesting insight into the writer's personal and professional life. Open 09:45–16:30, Mon–Fri; 11:00–16:30, Sat and holidays.

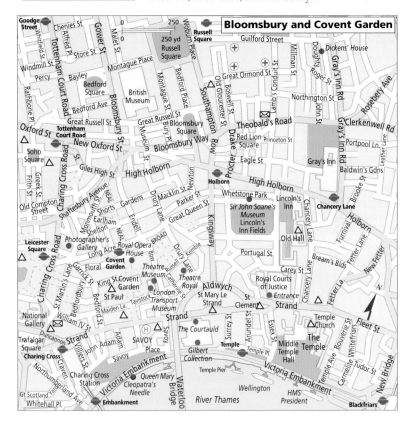

**Bloomsbury and Covent Garden**

**Left:** *The British Museum's collections were largely built up in the days of the Empire.*

### British Museum ★★★

The British Museum never fails to astound one but, given its size, plan for more than one visit. The extraordinary collections span from prehistoric times to the present day. Founded in the late 18th century, the museum has some seven and a half million exhibits in 88 galleries, requiring a walk of several miles to cover them all. It is one of the country's biggest tourist attractions – and entry is free.

The museum's great strengths are its collections of treasures and artworks from ancient Egypt, Greece and Rome, as well as Asia and the Far East, in addition to superb treasures from Roman and Anglo-Saxon Britain.

It's impossible to digest it all at once, and you might like to opt for one of the guided tours (four daily), which cover many of the highlights. Open 10:00–17:00, Monday–Saturday; 12:00–18:00, Sunday. For bookings, tel: (020) 7636 1555.

Treasures include the Rosetta Stone (dating from 196BC, it unlocked the language of ancient Egypt), mummies of the Pharaohs in the Egyptian Galleries; the human-headed lions and bulls of ancient Assyria; the Elgin Marbles and other Greek masterpieces; the Portland Vase with its exquisitely carved blue and white glass; the Lindow Man (sacrificed during a Druidic ceremony, his well-preserved body was found in peat in 1984), and the Sutton Hoo Anglo-Saxon treasures.

---

**THE GREAT COURT**

The British Museum is undergoing a transformation, due to be completed in November/ December 2000. The museum was home to the British Library (which has now moved to a new building alongside St Pancras Station) and the famous **Round Reading Room** (where Marx, Lenin and many other luminaries have studied) will be accessible to the general public for the first time in history – with computers now joining the reference books. The **Great Court** in which it stands is re-opening to the public for the first time since 1857, as a great covered square at the heart of the museum. It will contain a multi-level cultural complex. Until recently the museum's ethnographic collection was set up elsewhere as the **Museum of Mankind**, but part of it is now again on view and space for the rest will be available when the Great Court is finished.

**Right:** *Covent Garden is always alive with street entertainers and musicians of all kinds.*
**Opposite:** *A fashionable part of London popular with tourists and Londoners alike, Covent Garden offers a wide choice of restaurants, cafés and wine bars.*

### LONDON'S FIRST POLICE FORCE

The licentiousness of Covent Garden during the 18th century, with its thinly disguised brothels and bawdy houses, led to the formation of the nation's first police force. A magistrate's court had been established in Bow Street in 1748 and two resident magistrates, Henry Fielding (author of *Tom Jones*) and his brother John, set up their own private force of six plain-clothes policemen who became known as the **Bow Street Runners**. Although they had some success in cleaning up prostitution, lawlessness still ruled: in 1770, the Prime Minister, Lord Chancellor and Prince of Wales were all robbed in broad daylight in the West End. Mounted patrols operated from Bow Street from 1805, but it wasn't until 1829 that a unified force, the Metropolitan Police, was finally created.

## COVENT GARDEN

At the core of Covent Garden is the **piazza** – London's oldest planned square – which was originally designed by Inigo Jones in the 1630s. It was a very desirable residential area until market traders started moving in, and later, insalubrious coffee houses, gambling dens and brothels sprang up around the piazza. The central **market hall** was built in the 1830s (the glass roof was added later) and continued to be the country's most important wholesale fruit and vegetable market until it was relocated to Vauxhall in 1974. Today the market hall, piazza and surrounding streets (particularly in the converted warehouses to the north) are crammed with speciality shops, restaurants, pubs and much more besides. It has become one of London's major tourist attractions. On the west side of the piazza is **St Paul's Church** – known as the 'Actors' Church' due to its proximity to theatreland – which has numerous memorials to famous actors and actresses. Appropriately enough, the space in front of the church is now the main venue for Covent Garden's **street entertainers**, with an almost non-stop parade of jugglers, mime artists, musicians and other buskers every day and night.

Facing Bow Street on the east side of the piazza is the **Royal Opera House**, home to the Royal Ballet and Opera. Built in the early 19th century, this grandiose building has recently reopened after major redevelopement.

## London Transport Museum **

One of the old market sheds on the east side houses the museum which traces the history of transport in the capital from old horse-drawn buses to trams, the underground (the world's oldest, begun in 1863), buses and much more. There are plenty of interactive exhibits (including a computer-simulated tube-train drive) and such things as old news items and posters can be viewed on computer screens. Open 10:00–17:15, Sat–Thurs; 11:00–17:15, Friday.

## Theatre Museum **

Round the corner in Russell Street is the Theatre Museum (open 10:00–17:30, Tuesday–Sunday) which contains memorabilia including theatre props, programmes and costumes from the world of ballet, theatre, circus and opera. There's also a display ('Slap'), of the history of stage make-up. Demonstrations are given six times daily (between 11:30 and 16:30), and you may be the person picked from the audience for a theatrical face make-up.

## Theatre Royal, Drury Lane *

This was one of the first theatres to be built in London after the end of Oliver Cromwell's puritanical rule (during which theatre-going was banned), and was completed in 1663. After a fire it was rebuilt in 1812, and remodelled again in 1921. The staircases and foyer feature an impressive range of statues and paintings of famous actors. An entertaining tour operates twice or three times daily, led by three actors who constantly change character and costume. It is designed to amuse as well as to educate, including history, ghosts and backstage areas. Tickets can be obtained from the box office but it is generally best to book ahead, tel: (020) 7494 5091. The theatre is known as Theatre Royal, Drury Lane, even though the entrance is on Catherine Street.

> ### MARKETS AND SHOPS
>
> The main market at Covent Garden is in the central **market hall**, mostly specializing in arts and crafts, but don't expect too many bargains. On the south side of the piazza the **Jubilee Hall market** offers mainly clothes and accessories. Stalls rotate regularly and on Mondays both areas feature antiques. In King Street is the Africa Crafts Centre, which also has an ethnic restaurant. Some of the most interesting shops are found in the pedestrianized area just to the north of the main piazza. Just off Short's Gardens, Neal's Yard is the main focal point for alternative culture in the area, with excellent vegetarian cafés, bakeries, a herbal shop, therapy centres and a shiatsu school.

## CLEOPATRA'S NEEDLE

On the Embankment opposite Victoria Gardens stands London's oldest monument, which is known as Cleopatra's Needle. This 18m (59ft) obelisk was originally one of a pair from Cleopatra's Palace outside Alexandria, and dates back nearly 3500 years. It was presented to Britain by Egypt's ruler in 1819, but it took another 60 years before it was finally erected on this spot – and even then the sphinxes which flank it were placed back to front.

A wit of the day coined the following ditty:

'This monument,
as some supposes,
Was looked upon
of old by Moses.
It passed in time
from Greek to Turks
And was stuck up here
by the Board of Works.'

**Below:** *Splendid Art Deco features add allure to the grand Savoy Hotel.*

## THE STRAND

Connecting Trafalgar Square with Fleet Street, the **Strand** was once on the waterfront, and in the late 19th century it was at the heart of London's theatreland. One of the few theatres left is the **Adelphi Theatre**, built in 1806 and remodelled in Art Deco style in the 1930s. On the south side of the Strand is the **Savoy Theatre**, adjoining the famous Savoy Hotel. Opened in 1889, the Savoy is one of the city's grandest hotels and its forecourt is the only street in the UK where traffic drives on the right. The impressive Art Deco **Thames Foyer** is well worth seeing; you can also enjoy a proper English tea in these elegant surroundings.

### Somerset House ★★★

Built in 1786, on the site of the palace of the Earls of Somerset, this imposing classical building was the first major building in the country to be designed as offices and is now one of the capital's most important showplaces for art. Open 10:00–18:00, Monday–Saturday; 12:00–18:00, Sunday.

One wing (entered from the Strand) now houses the **Courtauld Gallery**, one of the finest collections of Impressionist and post-Impressionist paintings in the country, in addition to many master painters from other eras and some sculptures and furniture.

The central courtyard features a 55-jet fountain, illuminated at night, and connects the Courtauld to a wing (with another entrance on Victoria Embankment, the first London thoroughfare to be lit by electricity – in 1879) that now houses the magnificent **Gilbert Collection**, a recently acquired 800-piece collection of decorative arts. There's a spectacular display of large ornamental objects in the main gallery: mostly featuring gold, silver and Italian mosaics, and a side gallery has a wealth (literally) of such small items as snuffboxes and miniatures – even a jewel encrusted Portuguese crown.

Due to open in November 2000 are the **Hermitage Rooms**, which will house an exhibition of different items on loan (probably permanent) from St Petersburg's Hermitage Museum.

**Above:** *Middle Temple Hall has a splendid Elizabethan hammerbeam roof and was the setting for the first performance of William Shakespeare's* Twelfth Night *in 1602.*

## The Inns of Court *

Near Bloomsbury and Covent Garden is the area which has been the focal point of the country's legal system since the 13th century. Here, potential lawyers studied, ate and slept at one of the four **Inns of Court** (Gray's Inn, Lincoln's Inn, Middle Temple and Inner Temple), and vestiges of this 'live-in' system of learning still persist today; barristers are required to eat a specified number of dinners here before they can qualify to practise at the Bar.

Interesting buildings include **Middle Temple Hall** with wood-panelled walls that date from the 16th century and portraits of Tudor kings and queens, and **Temple Church**, built in 1185 by the Knights Templar and featuring stone effigies of Crusaders. Both are open to the public when not in use for functions.

## Sir John Soane's Museum **

On the north side of Lincoln's Inn Fields, this museum is one of London's best kept secrets. Based on the personal accumulation of art works and antiques of architect Sir John Soane, this unusual collection includes works by Hogarth, Reynolds, Turner and Canaletto, and many of his architectural drawings. In the basement of this intriguing house is the Egyptian sarcophagus of Seti I. Open 10:00–17:00, Tuesday–Saturday.

---

**ROYAL COURTS OF JUSTICE**

This imposing building on the Strand is open to visitors 09:00–16:30, Monday–Friday, October–July. There is a display of legal robes and, more importantly, you can visit one of the 79 courts to see British justice in action.

# 5
# West and Southwest London

Separated from Notting Hill and Bayswater by the green expanse of Hyde Park, the Royal Borough of **Kensington** still has an air of exclusivity about it, although it is no longer the aristocratic suburb it was over 100 years ago. **Kensington Palace**, a royal residence, adjoins **Kensington Gardens** and **Hyde Park**, which together form London's largest park. To the south, **Knightsbridge** is a smart residential area – the famous **Harrods** store its main attraction.

Several of London's top museums are located in **South Kensington** ('South Ken' to Londoners), with the **Victoria and Albert**, **Natural History** and **Science museums** next door to each other. These are the legacy of the 1851 **Great Exhibition of the Works of Industry of All Nations**, keenly promoted by Prince Albert, Queen Victoria's consort. It featured a unique wrought-iron and glass 'Crystal Palace' as its centrepiece, filled with exhibits from around the world. On the southern side of Hyde Park, the Crystal Palace drew over six million visitors and the Exhibition's profits were used to buy 35ha (87 acres) of land nearby to create a 'Museumland' that would promote the arts and sciences. This led to the creation of South Kensington's museums. The palace was torn down and reconstructed in southeast London, where it burned down in 1936.

Neighbouring **Chelsea** features many tranquil mews houses and prime residential streets, such as Cheyne Walk on the banks of the Thames. However, its best-known thoroughfare is **King's Road**, birthplace of the 'Swinging Sixties', and still one of London's fashion Meccas.

**DON'T MISS**

**\*\*\* The museums of South Kensington:** Natural History, Science and V&A.
**\*\* King's Road:** the fashion parade in trendy **Chelsea**.
**\*\* Hyde Park:** walk, picnic, or jog – or hire a row boat on the Serpentine.
**\*\* Notting Hill Carnival:** the exuberant carnival in August.
**\* Knightsbridge:** window-shopping in **Harrods** and **Harvey Nichols**.
**\* Albert Memorial:** Victorian Gothic Splendour.
**\* Queensway:** Edwardian Whiteleys and Queens Ice Bowl.

**Opposite:** *The richly decorated exterior of the Natural History Museum, which opened in 1881.*

## WHITELEYS

In 1885, William Whiteley opened the country's first real department store and, in 1896, Queen Victoria granted it a Royal Warrant. It went into decline after WWII, but reopened in 1989, having been restored to its Edwardian glory. Nowadays the lower floors are filled with shops, while the upper floors are for entertainment, with an eight-screen cinema, restaurants varying from Chinese to Tex-Mex and changing art exhibitions. The complex is open from 09:00–24:00 daily. Most shops open 10:00–22:00 Mon–Sat, 12:00–18:00 Sun.

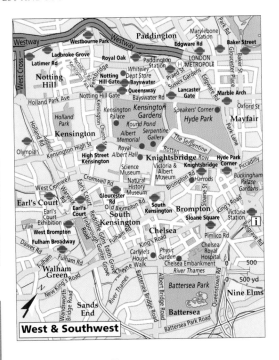

**West & Southwest**

## NOTTING HILL CARNIVAL

From Saturday through to Monday on the August Bank Holiday weekend every year, Notting Hill heaves with hundreds of thousands of people celebrating the famous **Carnival** – ear-splitting reggae, Caribbean soca, hip-hop and other music booms out from dozens of sound systems set up in the streets. The main events are the costume parades on Sunday and Monday, and the steel band contest on Saturday, with massive, colourful floats inching their way around a 2km (1¼ miles) circuit of Notting Hill. There are also several stages for live music, and stalls everywhere selling Red Stripe, Jamaican patties and other exotica. The nearest fully operational tube is usually Westbourne Park.

## NOTTING HILL AND BAYSWATER

To the north and northwest of Hyde Park respectively, both Bayswater and Notting Hill are characterized by the contrast of smart terraces and sweeping crescents alongside rather down-at-heel areas, with similarly cosmopolitan populations – in the case of Bayswater, largely Arabic and Chinese communities, and in Notting Hill mostly Afro-Caribbean.

### Queensway *

With Hyde Park at its southern end, Queensway is a hive of activity, offering lots of eateries which span the world's cuisines. There are fast food places, patisseries, ice-cream parlours, 'Eat as much as you like' joints and restaurants with live entertainment – many stay open late, as do some of the shops. At No. 17 is **Queens Ice Bowl**, home to London's only **ice-skating rink** and **ten-pin bowling** alleys.

## Notting Hill *

Notting Hill was one of the first areas in the capital (along with Brixton, Stockwell and Tottenham) to receive an influx of immigrants from the Caribbean in the post-war period, in this case primarily from Trinidad and Barbados. Already a poor slum area, it witnessed the country's first race riots in 1958 when competition for jobs and housing with white residents spilled over into violence. Partly to re-assert their Afro-Caribbean identity, the first **Notting Hill Carnival** was organized by the community in the early 1960s, based on the Trinidadian tradition of street carnivals. Held every August Bank Holiday, it is now Europe's biggest street festival, attracting upwards of a million spectators, and the largest carnival in the world apart from Rio.

The other main attraction in Notting Hill is the extensive **Portobello Road market**, at its best Saturday, featuring everything from antiques to clothing and even food, in an environment bursting with atmosphere.

## HYDE PARK

London's largest park, Hyde Park was originally a hunting ground for Henry VIII, and was first opened to the public during the reign of James I. Together with adjoining Kensington Gardens it provides a massive open space (covering 250ha/618 acres) in the heart of the city, a haven for dog-walkers, joggers, horseriders, skateboarders and cyclists (as might be imagined, conflict between these different groups is common).

At the centre of the park is the **Serpentine**, a long, artificial lake popular for rowing (rowboats can be hired). There is also a swimming club at the Serpentine, and members pride themselves on swimming all through the year, especially

---

### THE TYBURN GALLOWS

The corner of Hyde Park where the Marble Arch now stands was the site of the infamous **Tyburn Gallows** until they were demolished in 1825. The gallows (also known as the 'Tyburn Tree') coped with the execution of over 20 people at a time, and the almost daily hangings drew enormous crowds. In 1740, one guide book to London proclaimed it to be one of the city's chief attractions. The condemned were brought from Newgate Prison by cart, sometimes with the noose already in place, and allowed a free drink at ale houses along the way before being tied to the fatal tree; the cart was then whipped away. At the time, over 150 offences (including such minor misdemeanours as petty theft) warranted a one-way ticket to Tyburn.

**Below:** *Portobello Road is one of London's biggest and busiest antique markets.*

**Right:** *Horse riding is popular in Hyde Park along Rotten Row (the name is a corruption of* route du roi*).*
**Below:** *Speaker's Corner at Marble Arch, where anyone who wishes may address the crowds.*
**Opposite:** *The food hall at Harrods, in Knightsbridge, London's most famous department store, where the emphasis is on quality.*

at Christmas. On the south side of the lake, the **Serpentine Gallery** holds interesting exhibitions, mostly of contemporary art. Open daily 10:00–18:00.

In Hyde Park's northeastern corner is **Marble Arch**, which was moved here in 1851 from outside Buckingham Palace.

Marble Arch stands on what is essentially one of two traffic islands split by a quiet bus lane at the west end of Oxford Street, but both have been greened up to form an extension to Hyde Park. Across from Marble Arch is **Speaker's Corner**, which has been a rallying point for political dissent since the 1850s, and is now best known for the soap-box orators who regularly entertain the crowds here (particularly on Sunday mornings) with their rantings and ravings.

Park Lane runs down the east side of the park, culminating in **Hyde Park Corner**, where **Constitution Arch** is also stranded in the middle of a busy traffic roundabout. On the northwest side of Hyde Park Corner is **Apsley House**, a remarkable mansion which was, once upon a time, the home of the Duke of Wellington (during his lifetime

the house was referred to as Number One, London).
Built by Robert Adam between 1771 and 1778, the house
was occupied by the 'Iron Duke' when he was at the
height of his career as the most powerful commander in
Europe, and the lavish interior fittings, furnishings and
paintings (which include works by Rubens, Velázquez,
Goya and Correggio) reflect his stature at the time.
Open 11:00–17:00, Tuesday–Sunday.

From Hyde Park Corner running past the southern
edge of the Serpentine is **Rotten Row**, a fashionable
bridlepath where the Household Cavalry exercise every
morning from their nearby barracks. Past here is the
**Albert Memorial**, opposite the **Royal Albert Hall** on
Kensington Gore (*see* p. 67).

## KNIGHTSBRIDGE

Knightsbridge and neighbouring Belgravia boast some of
the priciest real estate in the capital, with numerous
embassies and exclusive hotels scattered throughout
their secluded squares. The main attraction for visitors,
however, is **Harrods** – a store which actually imposes a
dress code: no shorts, ripped jeans
or vest tops – on Brompton Road.
More than 30,000 people pass
through its doors every day to
shop in one of 300 departments
spread over seven floors; its post-
Christmas sale attracts 10 times
that many people. If your time is
limited, don't miss the Art Deco
food halls on the ground floor.
It is open 10:00–19:00, Mon–Sat.
Nearby **Harvey Nichols** (known
as 'Harvey Nicks' to its regular
customers) is another top department store much favoured by the
Sloane set. It is open 10:00–19:00,
Monday, Tuesday and Saturday;
10:00–20:00, Wednesday, Thursday
and Friday; 12:00–18:00, Sunday.

### HARRODS

This internationally famous
store, which was originally a
tea-dealer's shop in the City,
moved into Knightsbridge
in 1849 and began selling
perfumes, medicines and
stationery, as well as gro-
ceries. By 1880 it employed
nearly 100 assistants, and in
1898 installed London's first
escalator – with a member
of staff standing at the top
ready to revive customers
with brandy and smelling
salts. The present building,
which is illuminated at night,
dates from 1905. Today,
Harrods employs over 3000
staff and is owned by the
Egyptian Al Fayed brothers.

**Opposite above:**
*Model boating is popular on the Round Pond in Kensington Gardens.*
**Below:** *Kensington Palace houses royal apartments but a part of it is also open to the public.*

## KENSINGTON
### Kensington Gardens ★★

The westerly extension of Hyde Park, Kensington Gardens were once the private grounds of Kensington Palace. The Gardens became a public park in 1841, and now merge seamlessly with Hyde Park itself. The delightful gardens feature several ornamental fountains and statues – the latter including Jacob Epstein's *Rima* as well as the famous statue of JM Barrie's fictional *Peter Pan* by George Frampton (dating from 1912) which has sculpted squirrels, mice, rabbits, birds and fairies cavorting at its base. The Round Pond, just near Kensington Palace, is very popular with children (and indeed adults) piloting model boats. The splendid playground in the park is a memorial to Diana, Princess of Wales, who lived in Kensington Palace until her tragic death in 1997.

### Kensington Palace ★★

Kensington Palace, at the western end of Kensington Gardens, was originally a modest country mansion before being transformed by William of Orange in 1689. The Palace currently provides apartments for Prince and Princess Michael of Kent, the Duke and Duchess of Gloucester, and Princess Margaret.

The **State Apartments** have recently reopened after a £2.5 million facelift; the main highlights are the **trompe l'oeil** galleries above the King's Staircase; the King's Gallery

(with works by Rubens and Van Dyck); Queen Victoria's Bedroom, where she woke one morning in June 1837 to find her uncle had died and she was Queen; and the Court Dress Collection. The State Apartments are open daily, 10:00–17:00 in summer; 10:00–16:00 in winter. Take tea in the superb (and expensive) **Orangery**, originally built for Queen Anne. Open daily from 10:00 until dusk.

**AROUND KENSINGTON**

**Kensington High Street** has a range of shops from department stores such as **Barkers** to small boutiques, and branches of major chains such as **Gap**. Running north from St Mary Abbots church is **Kensington Church Street** which specializes in antiques. You'll find several good French patisseries and bakeries near the **Institut Français** (Cromwell Place) in South Kensington.

## The Commonwealth Institute*

The Commonwealth Institute, situated at the western end of Kensington High Street, houses changing exhibitions relating to the 54 Commonwealth countries. For current details, tel: (020) 7603 4535.

## Holland Park ★★

This charming park covers just 22ha (54 acres) but within it there are woodland areas (at their best in May, when the azaleas and rhododendrons are in bloom), rose gardens, formal flower gardens, an iris garden and a Japanese garden (created for the 1991 London Festival of Japan). The park, open from 7:30 until dusk throughout the year, was once the private garden of 17th-century Holland House, largely destroyed by Nazi bombing in World War II. The remains of the house now contain a youth hostel and restaurant (in the former orangery), whilst the terrace is used as an open-air theatre during summer. In Holland Park Road is **Leighton House**, a fascinating building crammed with art treasures. Open 11:00–17:15, Wednesday–Monday.

**Below:** *Holland Park, although not large, includes impressive gardens and blooms.*

**Above:** *The V&A charts the history of art and design through the ages.*
**Opposite:** *Modelled on a Roman amphitheatre, the Royal Albert Hall is one of the capital's largest concert halls.*

---

**THE GREAT EXHIBITION**

The Great Exhibition of 1851 was visited by 6 million people and the profits were used to buy 35ha (86 acres) of land in South Kensington, where Prince Albert's vision of a metropolis for the Science and Arts was created. Besides the museums themselves, other insitutions which were developed include the Royal Geographical Society, the Royal College of Organists, and the headquarters of the Royal College of Art.

---

## SOUTH KENSINGTON

Situated between Knightsbridge and Kensington is South Kensington, an area renowned for its high Victorian architecture and three of the world's best museums.

### Victoria and Albert Museum ★★★

Housing the world's largest collection of decorative art and design pieces, the huge Victoria and Albert Museum usually requires more than just one visit. Founded with proceeds from the Great Exhibition of 1851, it is generally known simply as the V&A. It is open 10:00–17:45, Thursday–Tuesday; 10:00–21:30, Wednesday.

The museum's 145 galleries house an extraordinary range of displays which include one of the world's most comprehensive jewellery collections, Europe's largest dress collection, major collections of British paintings, sculptures, musical instruments and furniture and the largest exhibition of Indian art outside India.

### Natural History Museum ★★★

The Romanesque-style exterior of the Natural History Museum on Exhibition Road may look forbidding, but the interior houses many interesting interactive exhibits and imaginative displays on the natural world – some geared specifically to children, although they are of course also an important resource for students and zoologists.

On entering the main building you are immediately confronted with a massive, 26m (83ft) skeleton of a *Diplodocus*, signalling one of the museum's major attractions for the younger generation, with their enduring fascination with dinosaurs. This is fully exploited in the superb **Dinosaur Gallery**. Other popular displays are **Creepy Crawlies** (with enlarged models of all sorts of insects, spiders and crustaceans) and **Ecology** (where all forms of life are found). Open 10:00–17:30, Monday–Saturday; 11:00–17:30, Sunday.

## Science Museum ★★★

Another colossus – best digested in manageable chunks – the Science Museum extends over seven floors. The original museum covered everything from transport to space travel and chemistry to telecommunications, with masses of interactive displays.

The new **Wellcome Wing** (opened June 2000) is an ultra-modern hi-tech extension where most of the exhibits are interactive. The basement **Launch Pad** is aimed at children, while adults can contribute to current research in the **Live Science** area and everyone can enjoy finding out about themselves in **Who Am I?** It includes a choice of 10-minute simulated rides and an **Imax** screen. Open 10:00–18:00 daily.

## Royal Albert Hall and Albert Memorial ★

The vast edifice of the **Royal Albert Hall** was completed in 1871 and since its completion has witnessed everything from rock concerts and religious revival meetings to tennis matches. Its most high-profile performances are now the annual Promenade Concerts.

Opposite the Royal Albert Hall, in Kensington Gardens, is the **Albert Memorial**, completed in 1876. It has a spire inlaid with semi-precious stones and a frieze depicting 169 life-size figures of scientists, painters, musicians, poets and architects. The memorial has recently been restored, returning it to its original Victorian Gothic splendour, adorned with gilded angels and bright mosaics. The seated figure of Prince Albert, holding a catalogue of the Great Exhibition, has been coated with two layers of gold leaf, as he was originally. Every figure has significance and there are guided 50-minute tours (which go inside the railings for close inspection) at 14:00 and 15:00 on Sundays.

**WILDLIFE GARDEN**

The Natural History Museum's first 'living exhibition' is in the form of a **Wildlife Garden**, intended as both an outdoor classroom and living laboratory. The single acre garden has 950 trees, 3800 shrubs, and 20,000 wildflowers, and is landscaped to recreate natural sites such as oak and bluebell woods, marshes and ponds, and wildflower meadows.

**THE PROMENADE CONCERTS**

From July to September each year the Royal Albert Hall hosts a series of virtuoso classical performances under the umbrella of the **Henry Wood Promenade Concerts** (usually known as 'the Proms'). The atmosphere is particularly lively on the famous Last Night of the Proms. Apply in writing for tickets, using BBC Proms Guide, available from bookshops and newsagents.

**SWINGING CHELSEA**

The first Continental-style coffee bar opened on the corner of Markham Street in the early 1960s, and the first boutique shortly thereafter; from these small beginnings King's Road grew into the focal point of the 'Swinging Sixties', a busy scene centred on fashion, music, and youth culture where you might well have bumped into the likes of Mick Jagger, David Bailey, Michael Caine, Jane Birkin, Mary Quant or George Best.

**Below:** *A typical street in Chelsea. One of London's smarter areas, it boasts many elegant townhouses.*

## CHELSEA

A short walk from either Knightsbridge or South Kensington, Chelsea has always been a mecca for dedicated followers of fashion. Chelsea is still one of *the* places to see and be seen, to shop – for everything from cult clubwear to classic brand-name clothes – and to spot famous rock stars, royalty or supermodels. It rose to fame in the 1960s with the arrival of 'Swinging London', when the 'Chelsea set' dictated fashion trends (the miniskirt being one of them) which the world followed. The pattern was repeated in the late 1970s, with the creation of punk. Chelsea still keeps abreast of the times, and many of London's sassiest young designers are based here today.

Running through the heart of Chelsea is **King's Road**, with **Sloane Square** at one end, and World's End at the other, chock-a-bloc with trendy shoe shops, indoor antique markets, fashion boutiques, bars and coffee shops. Although perhaps not as star-studded now as it once was, it is still a fun place to be – particularly on Saturday afternoons, when it is at its busiest. King's Road was initially a farmers' track which passed through Chelsea's market gardens. It later became a private royal thoroughfare used by King Charles II as a way of avoiding carriage congestion when visiting his mistress, Nell Gwynne, in Fulham. It was most likely a short cut to Hampton Court.

Chelsea is also famous for its Royal Hospital, the grounds of which house the annual Chelsea Flower Show.

Just across either the beautiful Albert Bridge or Battersea Bridge, on the other side of the Thames, is Battersea, which underwent considerable gentrification in the 1980s. Today, with Battersea Park at its heart, it boasts many little wine bars and smart shops.

**Left:** *Chelsea Pensioners, in their characteristic scarlet uniforms and medals, are part of the Chelsea landscape.*

---

**EARLS COURT**

Southwest of Kensington is Earls Court, a lively area where it's possible to find reasonable-cost accomodation and cheap eating places. It is also home to a vast stadium where exhibitions of all types are staged.

---

## Chelsea Embankment *

One of the most famous addresses in Chelsea is **Cheyne Walk**, whose Georgian and Queen Anne houses looked right over the Thames until the building of the Embankment in 1874. Among the many celebrities who have lived here are novelists Henry James (No. 21) and George Eliot (No. 4); pre-Raphaelite painter Dante Gabriel Rossetti (No. 16); artists Whistler (No. 93) and Turner (No. 118) and, more recently, pop stars Mick Jagger (No. 48) and Keith Richard (No. 3). Just around the corner at 24 Cheyne Row is **Carlyle's House** where historian Thomas Carlyle's personal effects have been kept as they were when he died in 1881. Open 11:00– 16:30, Wednesday–Sunday, and holiday Monday Easter–Oct.

---

**THOMAS MORE**

The 16th-century scholar and statesman **Thomas More**, martyred by Henry VIII in 1535, was a long-term resident of Chelsea. He is commemorated by a statue on the Chelsea Embankment, at the end of Cheyne Walk.

---

## Chelsea Physic Garden **

One of the great delights of Chelsea is this little-known garden in Royal Hospital Road. It marks the beginning of Cheyne Walk and is the second oldest botanical garden in England after Oxford's. It was founded by the Society of Apothecaries in 1673 and used to teach physicians the medicinal uses of plants and herbs from all over the world. The Chelsea Physic Garden contains over 5000 plants, including the UK's largest outdoor olive tree. At the entrance, maps are available with a list of the most interesting flowers and shrubs. Open 12:00–17:00, Wednesday, 14:00–18:00 Sunday, April–October.

---

**CHELSEA SHOPS**

King's Road is no longer as fashionable as it was in the 1960s, but there are still lots of top name shops here, as well as some good pubs and restaurants. Signs of the times are a branch of Marks and Spencer and a Safeway supermarket. Further west, towards World's End, are a number of antique shops.

# 6
# The City, the East End and Docklands

The City of London, as it is known, is London's commercial and financial heartland. The area, steeped in history, includes many famous sights and institutions, including the Bank of England, the Royal Exchange, the Stock Exchange, the Monument to the Great Fire of London, the Central Criminal Court at the Old Bailey and the Mansion House, which is the residence of the Lord Mayor of London (*see* p. 16).

The most enduring legacy from medieval times is the fascinating **Tower of London**, begun by William the Conqueror and completed in the 14th century. Along with Christopher Wren's masterpiece – **St Paul's Cathedral** – the Tower is not to be missed.

Fuelled by deregulation of financial services in the 1980s, the City underwent a building boom which resulted in developments such as the **Broadgate Centre** and the controversial **Lloyd's of London** building (*see* p. 75).

**The East End** is traditionally a working class district where the main attractions are the excellent markets.

To the east of the City is the area known as **Docklands**, best viewed from a pleasure boat coursing up the Thames. Not the most obvious of tourist attractions within the capital, it is nevertheless a fascinating area – not least because it is the largest urban regeneration project in the world, a status symbolized by the domineering presence of Cesar Pelli's 245m (803ft) high **Canary Wharf Tower**, Britain's tallest building and the second highest in Europe, beaten only by Frankfurt's Messeturm – but if current planning applications are approved the skyline will change.

### DON'T MISS

**\*\*\* Tower of London:** an interesting guided tour, led by Beefeaters, including the **Crown Jewels**.
**\*\*\* Tower Bridge:** views from this walkway as well as the Golden Gallery at the top of **St Paul's Cathedral**.
**\*\* Museum of London:** charts the fascinating history of London.
**\*\* Docklands:** ride on the elevated railway to Greenwich.
**\* Markets:** the bustling East End at weekends.

**Opposite:** *Night-time illuminations reveal the grand façade of St Paul's.*

**Above:** *The Royal Exchange. The City is a major centre for international business.*

## THE CITY

The City of London, often called the 'Square Mile' is contained more or less within the area that was originally covered by Roman Londinium. It was almost destroyed in the Great Fire of 1666 and suffered again in the Blitz of 1940, but there is still plenty of interest to see. Although full of modern buildings, the City's streets and alleys still largely follow the Medieval layout.

### St Paul's Cathedral ★★★

St Paul's presents a magnificent façade from the west side, with its two baroque towers capped by a 111m (364ft) dome (second only in size to St Peter's in Rome). Wren's airy design is immediately apparent on entering (open 08:30–16:00, Monday–Saturday), with the impressive dome featuring a series of trompe l'oeil frescos on the life of St Paul. In the north aisle of the nave is a bronze and marble monument to the Duke of Wellington. In the North Transept is Holman Hunt's *The Light of the World*.

The enormous, brightly lit crypt is reached via a flight of stairs in the South Transept, and contains some 350 memorials and over 100 tombs. Recent additions include a memorial to British troops who died in the Falklands, but pride of place goes to the tombs of Wellington and Nelson. Artists (such as Turner and Reynolds) are buried here, as is scientist Alexander Fleming, and Wren himself, whose

The City

epitaph reads: '*reader, if you seek his monument, look around you*'. The first of the three galleries under the dome is the Whispering Gallery; the second is the Stone Gallery, and the third the Golden Gallery (627 steps up) with fabulous views over the City.

South of St Paul's the innovative **Millennium Bridge** will provide a direct pedestrian link to Tate Modern.

## Fleet Street *

Once the home of most of Britain's national newspapers, Fleet Street was a popular haunt of scribes and clerks from the 15th century onwards. In 1702 Britain's first daily newspaper, the *Daily Courant*, was published here, and from the 19th century onwards nearly every major paper had printing presses in the vicinity.

Behind the Reuters building you'll find **St Bride's**, known as the 'journalists' church', which was designed by Wren and contains a small museum of Fleet Street history. Open 08:00–16:45, Monday–Saturday. Just off Fleet Street to the north in Gough Square is **Dr Johnson's House**, which was home to the great writer and lexicographer from 1747–59. The house contains some rather unusual memorabilia as well as etchings and portraits of Dr Johnson and his biographer, Boswell. Open 11:00–17:00, Monday–Saturday.

## The Barbican Complex *

This large, concrete-clad residential complex was built in the 1970s. At the heart of it is the **Barbican Arts Centre** (a confusing warren covering 12 levels, three of them underground), which is home to the Royal Shakespeare Company, the London Symphony Orchestra, the Guildhall School of Music and Drama, cinemas and a concert hall. For details and times of performances, tel: (020) 7638 8891.

**Below:** *The ceiling of St Paul's Cathedral, by Wren, is one of London's most familiar sights and merits a leisurely visit.*

**Museum of London ★★**

Adjacent to the Barbican Complex, the Museum
of London features 14 galleries charting the
history of the capital from prehistoric times up to
the present, with appropriate sound effects.
The museum also presents lectures, films and
special events.

The museum displays the history of London
from prehistoric times, beginning with a walk
along mud-paved streets, and offers a most
impressive account of the Roman era in its **Roman
Gallery**, where objects include the latest archaeo-
logical finds from around the City, mosaics,
sculptures, recreations of a Roman street and the
interior of ordinary houses, as well as models of
public baths, a forum and the old fort.

On the same floor the tale continues in chronological
order through medieval times to the Great Fire of London in
1666, highlights include the **Cheapside Hoard** (spectacular
jewellery spanning several centuries), a model of the **Globe**
theatre and the **Great Fire Experience** (a small diorama with
a tape of diarist Samuel Pepys's first-hand account).

Downstairs (passing the entrance to a lovely little
**Nursery Garden**) the display begins with the Stuart period
and continues to the 20th century. Exhibits here include
costumes and music from various periods, recreated
shops and offices, a pub, posters, paintings, all sorts of
bric-a-brac, an **Art Deco lift** from Selfridges and various
carriages, including the gilded **Lord Mayor's Coach**. Open
10:00–17:50, Monday–Saturday; 12:00–17:50 Sunday.

**Guildhall ★**

In the heart of the City, the Guildhall has been
London's administrative centre for over 800 years and
still houses the offices of the Corporation of London.
The Great Hall (10:00–16:30 weekdays) features coats of
arms and banners from the City's guilds and livery
companies. The **Guildhall Art Gallery** (open 10:00–17:00,
Mon–Sat; 12:00–16:00 Sun) houses the corporation's
paintings from the 17th to 20th centuries.

## Lloyd's of London *

Lloyd's of London started out as a society of underwriters who met in a City coffee house (after which the company took its name), and is now one of the world's biggest insurance underwriters. This avant-garde steel and glass building, designed by Richard Rogers, caused something of a stir when it was first unveiled in 1986.

## The Tower of London ***

One of the capital's most popular attractions, the Tower of London is a well-preserved medieval fortress which in its heyday housed around 1500 people. Over the last 900 years it has been a royal palace, a prison, an execution site, an armoury, and is today a repository for the Crown Jewels. Open 09:00–17:00 Mon–Sat and 10:00–17:00 Sun in summer; 09:00–16:00 Tues–Sat and 10:00–16:00 Sun and Mon in winter. The Yeoman Warders (Beefeaters) conduct frequent (free) tours which are both informative and amusing, so highly recommended – you can join and leave the groups at will, so make your own pace.

### DICK WHITTINGTON

The pantomime character of Dick Whittington, with his knapsack and cat, was based on the life of Richard Whittington, a wealthy merchant who first became Mayor of London in 1397. He was a great public benefactor and when he died, childless, in 1423, his fortune was bequeathed to civic works. By the 1500s his rags-to-riches story had become a legend, with Whittington (and his cat) poised to leave the city when he hears the Bow bells ring out 'turn again, Whittington, thrice Lord Mayor of London'. In fact, he was Mayor four times: a stone on Highgate Hill commemorates the spot where he is supposed to have heard the bells. There is also a stained glass window in his honour in St Michael Paternoster Royal in Skinner's Lane in the City.

**Opposite:** *Lloyd's of London is an architectural landmark in the heart of the City.*
**Left:** *The Tower of London was used to house prisoners from medieval times.*

**BEEFEATERS AND RAVENS**

The Tower of London was the city's first zoo, with leopards, elephants, birds and polar bears on display in medieval times. In the 19th century this menagerie was transferred to London Zoo, but the ravens – feeding on scraps from the palace kitchens and, it is said, pecking away at severed heads from executions – stayed on. An old legend has it that 'only so long as they stay will the White Tower stand' and since Charles II's time they have been protected by royal decree.

The centre of the complex is the **White Tower**, which dates back to the time of William the Conqueror. Inside are displays of arms and armour, including some used by Henry VIII. There is also an exhibition of torture instruments along with an axe and block used for executions at the Tower. On the first floor is the beautiful 11th century **St John's Chapel**, the oldest church in London.

In the northeastern corner is the **Martin Tower**, which houses an exhibition, Crowns and Diamonds, which includes some rare 18th and 19th century crown frames used at coronations.

Many prisoners arrived at the Tower by boat, entering via the **Traitor's Gate** before being incarcerated in one of the many fortified towers surrounding Tower Green, in the middle of the complex. Situated directly behind the Traitor's Gate is the **Bloody Tower**, where 12-year-old Edward V and his 10-year-old brother, the Duke of York, were (allegedly) murdered on the orders of Richard III. On the west side of the Bloody Tower is the **Queen's House** (now the home of the Tower's Governor and closed to the public) which was built by Henry VIII and used as a prison for Katherine Howard, Anne Boleyn and Lady Jane Grey; the last inmate was Hitler's Deputy, Rudolph Hess.

Nearby is **Tower Green**, the site of several executions, and the spot is marked by a plaque listing the

**Above:** *Beefeaters have been guarding the Tower since Henry VIII's time.*
**Right:** *The Queen's House in the Tower of London.*
**Opposite:** *The road across Tower Bridge is still raised periodically to allow ships to pass underneath.*

names of the victims. These include two of Henry VIII's wives, Anne Boleyn and Katharine Howard, Lady Jane Grey, the nine day queen, and the Earl of Essex, Elizabeth I's favourite. Behind is the church of **St Peter ad Vincula**, where they were all buried, without any memorial.

On the northern side of the compound the **Crown Jewels** are on display in the Waterloo Barracks. A moving walkway system carries you past them at a fairly fast pace. The sparkling exhibits include the Crown of State (bedecked with thousands of jewels including a 317-carat diamond), the Koh-i-Noor diamond, sceptres, orbs and other glittering regal paraphernalia.

## Tower Bridge **

Tower Bridge is a marvel of Victorian engineering (it took eight years to build) and was first opened to traffic on 30 June 1894. It was designed so that tall sailing ships could reach the Port of London – ships still have precedence over road traffic, although compared to the early years (when it was raised over 6000 times a year) it is seldom raised: only about 550 times a year. The 1000 ton bascules were originally raised using pure hydraulic power, but electricity is used today.

The bridge was built in the Gothic style to blend in with the Tower of London, but beneath its stonework exterior is a massive steel frame which you can see when you get inside. **Tower Bridge Experience** tours lead through a series of displays (including an animatronic Cockney bridge painter) on the bridge's history. Views from the top walkways are terrific. Tours start 10:00–17:15 daily in summer; 09:30–16:45 daily in winter.

---

**CEREMONIES AT THE TOWER**

The 700-year-old traditional **Ceremony of the Keys** takes place nightly at 21:53, as the Chief Yeoman Warder locks the Tower gates and performs a ritual exchange which has remained unchanged since Queen Elizabeth I's reign. For tickets to witness this ancient ceremony, write two months in advance to HM Tower of London, London EC3N 4AB, enclose an SAE and names and addresses of all group members. **Royal Gun Salutes** mark royal birthdays and other state occasions. The **Beating of the Bounds,** which takes place every three years on Ascension Day (the next time it takes place is in 2001), is also medieval in origin (the idea was to define the parish boundaries).

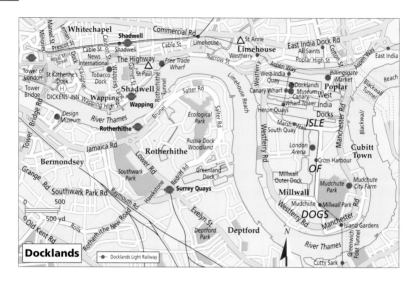

**Docklands**

Docklands Light Railway

## THE EAST END AND DOCKLANDS

The East End has a colourful past and has been a focal point for immigrants and refugees, from the Huguenots through to Irish, Jews, and Bengalis. Recently, the East End has acquired a new lease of life as a focus for contemporary art, with hundreds of artists living and working in the area (including the *enfant terrible* of the contemporary art world, Damien Hirst). Several influential galleries are located here, including the famed Whitechapel Art Gallery.

### Street Markets *

Of all the markets in this area, one of the best-known is in **Petticoat Lane** (mostly clothing), which has existed for over 200 years. Just to the north is the **Spitalfields market**, once the centre of the fruit and vegetable trade (now mostly crafts and food). East of here and at the heart of London's Bengali community, **Brick Lane** market (bric-a-brac and clothes) tempts passers-by with the aroma of curry wafting out from behind the stalls. **Columbia Road** is an enjoyable street filled with plant and flower stalls. All these markets are best on the weekends. The nearest tube stations are Liverpool Street and Aldgate East.

---

**DECLINE OF THE DOCKS**

Most of the dock system was built from the 19th century onwards, with the biggest docks being the vast Royal Docks, each 1.6km (5½ miles) long, with massive warehouses protected behind high walls to keep out thieves. The development of containerized shipping (for which a new port was built at Tilbury in the 1960s) and other factors eventually led to all the docks being shut down between 1968 and 1981. The area became an urban wasteland until regeneration began in the 1980s, when the London Docklands Development Corporation (LDDC) was set up, and developers moved into the new Enterprise Zone. Today, there are over 2000 businesses in the area.

## Whitechapel Art Gallery ★

One of London's top contemporary art galleries is in the heart of the East End: the Whitechapel Art Gallery was founded by a Victorian philanthropist and today often stages unusual exhibitions of avant-garde art from around the world. Open 11:00–17:00, Tuesday, Thursday–Sunday; 11:00–20:00, Wednesday.

## Bethnal Green Museum of Childhood★

The museum, in Cambridge Heath Road, houses a superb collection of toys and games past and present, including teddy bears, doll's houses and puppets. Open 10:00–17:50, Saturday–Thursday.

## Docklands ★

Best known for its hotchpotch of architectural styles, Docklands offers charming riverside pubs, restored warehouses, sailing ships, and even the urban **Mudchute Farm**, where you can go horse riding. Docklands is a catch-all term for a vast area extending east from London Bridge along the Thames, covering 22km² (8½ sq miles), bigger than the City of London and West End combined, with over 88km (55 miles) of waterfront. **St Katherine's Dock**, east of the Tower, has a marina, old swing bridges and an 18th-century pub, the **Dickens' Inn**. Further east, Limehouse, where the city's first Chinese community settled, is home to Hawksmoor's **St Anne's Church**, Commercial Road, distinguished by its church clock: the highest in the City. The Isle of Dogs is now the commercial hub of Docklands and West India Docks is home to the massive **Canary Wharf** development, as well as the new **Docklands Museum**. Open in September 2001, this will cover the history of the river and area since Roman times. Beyond are the Royal Docks and London City Airport.

---

**VISITING DOCKLANDS**

One of the best ways to see the new developments in Docklands is to take a boat trip from Westminster, Charing Cross or Tower piers to Greenwich. To get into the heart of Docklands take the Docklands Light Railway (DLR) from Bank or Tower Gateway station. The DLR is a fully automated, elevated rail system transporting some 110,000 people every day. Cutty Sark station is the best place to get off if you want to see the sights at Greenwich (Greenwich station itself is far less convenient for these). Alternatively, you may prefer to alight at Island Gardens and then walk the rest of the way through a tunnel under the Thames.

**Below:** *St Katherine's Dock was one of the first of the old docks to undergo redevelopment.*

# 7
# North London

The dividing line between Central and North London follows the busy traffic route of Marylebone and Euston Roads. Once known as New Road, this was the city's first bypass, built in 1756 to allow cattle to be herded from west of the city to Smithfield market without clogging up Oxford Street. The main attraction on Marylebone Road is **Madame Tussaud's** waxworks museum, one of London's most popular sights; you can combine a visit to Madame Tussaud's with the **Planetarium** next door.

North of Marylebone Road is **Regent's Park**, laid out in the early 1800s and home to **London Zoo** since 1834. Winding its way around the park's northern edge and passing through the zoo itself is the **Regent's Canal**, built to link the Grand Junction Canal at Paddington (which led in turn to the thriving industrial north) with the docks.

Beyond Regent's Park is elegant **Hampstead**, whose village-like atmosphere has appealed to artists, writers and celebrities of all kinds for many years. Spreading in a great swathe northwards from Hampstead is **Hampstead Heath**, one of the largest open spaces in the capital encompassing a range of landscapes including untamed woodland, ponds and lakes, meadows and fields. It is a popular venue for all sorts of activities, including open-air concerts at the historic **Kenwood House**.

To the east of Hampstead lies **Camden Town**, one of the capital's favourite weekend venues, with a vast network of market stalls sprawling around the Regent's Canal at Camden Lock. Both **Islington** and **Clerkenwell**, further east, are well worth a visit.

---

**DON'T MISS**

**\*\*\* Regent's Park:** a walk along the canalside combined with a visit to **London Zoo**, rowing on the lake or a visit to the **Open Air Theatre**.
**\*\*\* Hampstead:** explore the village and the wild spaces of **Hampstead Heath**.
**\*\* Camden:** catch up on the latest fashions in the busy weekend markets here.
**\*\* Madame Tussaud's:** incredible waxworks display.
**\* Camden Passage:** browse through the antique stalls and shops.

---

**Opposite:** *One of London's many famous graveyards, Highgate Cemetery features an array of unusual statuary.*

**Above:** *Queen Elizabeth I, one of hundreds of wax dummies at the renowned Madame Tussaud's.*
**Below:** *Madame Tussaud's and the Planetarium are among London's most popular attractions, so expect long queues for tickets, which can be avoided by getting a ticket in advance.*

## MARYLEBONE
### Madame Tussaud's ★★

One of the most popular tourist attractions in the capital, this famous waxworks museum attracts two to three million visitors annually and you should expect to queue a long time for tickets. It is possible to avoid the worst queue by purchasing tickets in advance: sources include the tourist buses.

Madame Tussaud's waxworks first came to London in 1802, after its eponymous creator was forced to flee the French Revolution, only narrowly escaping the guillotine herself by moulding death masks of the Revolution's victims. Madame Tussaud died in 1850 at the age of 89, and her last work, a self-portrait, is on display in the museum today. Open 09:00–17:30 daily, June–August; 10:00–17:30 Monday–Friday and 09:30–17:30 Saturday–Sunday, September–May.

The theme settings for the more than 400 waxwork figures within the complex start off with a **Garden Party**, where contemporary celebrities (such as Dudley Moore, Mel Gibson, Arnold Schwarzenegger and Dame Edna Everage) socialize in a replica of the grounds of an English country house. You can take your photo with your favourites. The **200 Years** display traces the history of modelling techniques from Madame Tussaud's first death mask of Marie Antoinette, through to the latest animatronic figures. **Legends** features stars of stage and screen, and leads through to the **Grand Hall**, where effigies of the Royal Family and world military leaders and statesmen stand proudly in full regalia.

The most popular section is undoubtedly the **Chamber of Horrors**, completely remodelled in 1996 to make it even more spine-chilling than it was before. Torture, dismemberment, and mass murderers such as Jack the Ripper are all on the menu here –

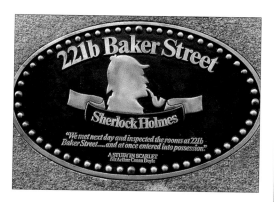

### LONDON CENTRAL MOSQUE

On the western edge of Regent's Park, the **London Central Mosque** attests to the continuing religious and architectural diversity of the capital. Completed in 1978, it has a shining copper dome, a minaret and traditional Islamic interior décor. It can accomodate 1800 worshippers. Non-Muslim visitors should start at the information centre.

although many of these scenarios are better presented in the London Dungeon (*see* p. 99). Finally, there is the **Spirit of London**, a journey through the history of the capital in miniaturized black taxi cabs. The tour starts in the court of Elizabeth I in the 16th century, continues through the Great Fire of London, the Industrial Revolution, the World War II Blitz and the Swinging London of the 60s.

### Planetarium ★★

The Planetarium, next door to Madame Tussaud's, is equally popular and a joint ticket is good value. Other than the main star shows, the Planetarium features exhibitions with models of planets, satellites and spacecraft, plus interactive demonstrations, and live weather pictures. The main auditorium features a 17-minute **Star Show**, using images from spacecraft and satellites woven together with a narrative on space travel, planets and the stars. Open 12:30–17:00, Monday–Friday; 10:00–17:00, Saturday and Sunday. Show every 40 minutes.

### Sherlock Holmes Museum ★

Sir Arthur Conan Doyle's fictional Victorian detective, Sherlock Holmes, had his home at 221b Baker Street. The Sherlock Holmes Museum is a faithful reconstruction of his house as it might have been. It is, in fact, located at 239 Baker Street, even though the sign on the door says otherwise. Open 09:30–18:30.

### REGENT'S CANAL

Running in a meandering path through north and east London down to the Thames at Limehouse, **Regent's Canal** was completed in 1820 and is still in use by narrowboats today. One of the most attractive sections is the small basin known as **Little Venice**, in Maida Vale (tube: Warwick Avenue) from where you can catch a **waterbus** down to **London Zoo** (which has its own jetty) and then on down to **Camden Lock**. The service runs hourly on the hour every day 10:00–17:00, Apr–Oct; Sat–Sun 10:00–15:00, Nov–Mar. Details from the London Waterbus Company, tel: (020) 7482 2550. **Jason's Canal Boats** do the same journey, with a commentary but without a zoo stop; tel: (020) 7286 3428.

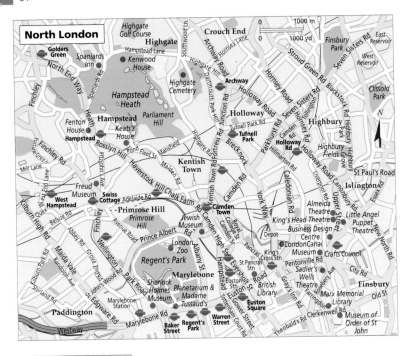

## REGENT'S PARK

Extending north from Marylebone Road up towards Hampstead and Camden, Regent's Park is best known as the home of London Zoo, and for the elegant Regency terraces (designed by John Nash) which surround it. It was once a thickly wooded area (and the private hunting grounds of Henry VIII) until Cromwell felled most of its 1600 trees to help build ships for the Navy.

Nash and the Prince Regent (later George IV) envisaged a belt of grand terraced houses around the outside of the park, and although the scheme was never completed, Nash's legacy is still visible in the cream-coloured stucco of **Chester Terrace** and **Cumberland Terrace**, and the architecturally diverse houses of **Park Village West**. The **Open-Air Theatre** in the Inner Circle was popular in the 1930s for its productions of *A Midsummer Night's Dream*, and the summer repertoire still includes

Shakespeare. The nearby **Queen Mary's Gardens** have one of the country's best rose displays. Beyond Prince Albert Row is **Primrose Hill**, well worth the climb to enjoy sweeping panoramas of the city.

## London Zoo **

Covering 14ha (34½ acres) of the northern corner of Regent's Park, the London Zoo has endured its fair share of ups and downs – including threats of complete closure due to funding problems – since it was first opened by the Zoological Society of London in 1828.

London Zoo is one of the world's oldest (built on a restricted site), and so cannot be compared with more modern zoos elsewhere in the world. It has, however, long been at the forefront of zoological studies and scientific research into animal genetics, ecology, behaviour, and reproduction, and can claim many firsts, including the public aquarium (1849), the reptile house (1853), the insect house (1881), and a children's zoo (1938).

The complex contains twelve listed buildings, including Mappin Terraces (intended to resemble a mountain landscape for sloth bears and other animals), the much-loved penguin pool, giraffe house and Snowdon Aviary.

But of course it is the animals that people come to see, and with 12,000 of them here there is plenty to observe and enjoy, from the tiniest tree snails in the invertebrate house to the Asian jumbos in the elephant house. Kids can feed and handle animals in the **Ambika Paul Children's Zoo**, watch the elephants being weighed, peer at possums and other creatures of the night in Moonlight World, ride on a camel, or watch a variety of birds and animals show off their special skills in the **Animals in Action** presentation. Open 10:00–17:30, daily in summer; 10:00–16:30 in winter.

> **CONSERVATION**
>
> London Zoo houses over 100 species which are facing extinction in the wild, and new projects invariably aim to educate the public about conservation. Such schemes as the successful 'Adopt an Animal' serve the dual functions of involving members of the public in a personal way and helping to provide funds for the zoo's upkeep and research.

**Below:** *The Snowdon Aviary rises up majestically alongside Regent's Canal at London Zoo.*

## CAMDEN TOWN

Another of London's more Bohemian 'village suburbs', Camden Town is popular among Londoners for its extensive **markets**, of which there are several at either side of **Camden Lock** on the Regent's Canal. You may well find designer clothes here before they become household names. At weekends it buzzes with activity and scores of shops, trendy pubs, bistros and restaurants complement the markets, each with their own character and style.

The original **Camden Market** has around 120 stalls where the emphasis is mostly on fashion, jewellery, and great second-hand clothing, music and food. Open 09:00–17:00, Thursday–Sunday. Between this market and Camden Town tube is the indoor **Electric Ballroom**, which operates as a market on Sundays only, and which features up-and-coming fashion and jewellery designers. Opposite here, the **Inverness Street Market** is the oldest section, and sells fruit and vegetables. Open Monday–Saturday.

On the other side of the canal bridge the **Camden Lock Market** (open daily), with many exotic food stalls, is the main arts and crafts area, with the many small boutiques and craft workshops supplemented at weekends by hundreds of stalls selling bric-a-brac, candles, prints, books, clothes, period clothing and much more besides.

Between Camden Town tube and Chalk Farm tube, **Camden High Street** and **Chalk Farm Road** (its extension) is the main drag, lined with a variety of interesting stores, from bookshops and galleries to specialist craft shops and plenty of trendy shoes, shades and clothes.

**Left:** *Camden Lock, terminus for canal cruises, is filled with little arty shops and stalls.*

**Opposite:** *St Pancras Station, one of London's most exuberant Victorian buildings.*

On Chalk Farm Road is the **Stables Antique Market** which is the biggest of all the markets, and has some of the best bargains in collectables and antiques, ornaments, furniture, and good quality second-hand clothes. It is open throughout the day on Saturdays and Sundays.

Within a few minutes' walk of Camden Town tube is the **Jewish Museum** at 129 Albert Street, which has a series of stylish galleries on Jewish history in Britain and religious life, and a renowned ceremonial art collection; there are also interesting audiovisual displays explaining the Jewish faith and customs. It includes treasures from London's Great Synagogue which was burnt down during the Second World War. Open 10:00–16:00, Sunday–Thursday; closed on Bank and Jewish holidays.

To the south of Camden Town the area around **King's Cross** railway station is a notorious red-light district, but it is due to be redeveloped as a terminal for the Channel tunnel trains. Alongside King's Cross the old **St Pancras** station, with its magnificent mock-Gothic spires, is a marvel of Victorian architecture. The much-criticized modern **British Library** is situated alongside it.

Behind King's Cross, canal boats moor up in the King's Cross Basin, where the interesting little **London Canal Museum** traces the social and commercial history of canal boats and the people who have lived and worked on them. Open 10:00–16:30, Tuesday–Sunday and bank holiday Mondays.

---

### THE BRITISH LIBRARY

After many delays, technical problems and overspending, the new British Library finally opened on Euston Road in 1997. It houses 12 million books, has 11 reading rooms and three exhibition spaces for the general visitor. Here are displayed such national treasures as two of the surviving four copies of *Magna Carta*, the First Folio of Shakespeare's works, the beautiful 7th century *Lindisfarne Gospels*, the original manuscript of Lewis Caroll's *Alice in Wonderland* and the score of Handel's *Messiah*. Open 09:30–18:00 Mon, Wed, Thurs, Fri; 09:30–20:00 Tue; 09:30–17:00 Sat; 11:00–17:00 Sun. For visitor information, tel: (020) 7412 7332.

**Above:** *The elegant, white-washed façade of Keats's former home in Hampstead.*

## HAMPSTEAD

Hampstead was first recorded in the Domesday Book as 'Hampstede', meaning homestead, and consisted of nothing more than a small rural farm. By the 18th century it had become a fashionable spa, selling water to city-dwellers in the aptly named **Flask Walk**, and later became (as it still is) a popular residence for the wealthy, the intelligentsia and literary set.

Hampstead's steeply sloping village **High Street** features numerous fashion shops, art and antiques galleries, boutiques and craft shops, as well as arty cafés and lively pubs. Surrounding it is a maze of cobblestone lanes, alleyways, elegant houses and Georgian squares.

### Hampstead Museums *

Before heading off to the wide open spaces of Hampstead Heath, there are several noteworthy museums in the vicinity. The **Freud Museum,** 20 Maresfield Gardens, (open 12:00–17:00, Wednesday–Sunday) is where Freud lived after escaping from the Nazis in 1938, until his death the following year. His library and study (including the famous couch) have been preserved and the house contains his collection of erotic antiquities and archives.

At **Keats's House**, Keats Grove, Wentworth Place, the poet is commemorated in the house where he lived 1818–20. The Regency villa contains a collection of his books, manuscripts, letters and personal possessions. It was here he created *Ode to a Nightingale* and fell in love with his neighbour, Fanny Brawne. Open 12:00–17:00, Tue–Sat; many special events 18:00–20:00 Wed.

Music aficionados should head for **Fenton House**, where the collection of old instruments includes a 1612 harpsichord played by Handel. Open 14:00–17:00 Wed and Fri; 11:00–17:00, Sat–Sun. Summer concerts on Thurs evenings. For information, tel: (01494) 755 563.

**SPANIARDS INN**

To the west of Kenwood House at the northern end of Spaniards Road, traffic is forced to slow down as it negotiates a narrow passage between an old toll booth and the historic **Spaniards Inn**, an 18th-century coaching inn. The famous highwayman Dick Turpin is said to have used it as a hiding place and to spy out likely looking coaches to rob as they left London on the road north. Legend has it that he would fire his pistol nightly as a signal at closing time.

## Hampstead Heath **

Hampstead's main attraction is the 300ha (741-acre) expanse of the Heath, one of the most popular parks in London, with woodlands, open fields, heath-land, and 28 natural ponds (some are used for swimming or fishing). For great views of Hampstead and the City head for **Parliament Hill**, which is a popular spot for kite-flying. On the northern fringes of the Heath is **Kenwood House**, a

17th-century mansion with a noteworthy interior re-modelled by Robert Adam – his library is a highlight. The house now contains the **Iveagh Bequest**, a fabulous collection featuring such artists as Vermeer, Rembrandt, Reynolds and Gainsborough. Open daily 10:00–18:00, Apr–Sept; 10:00–17:00, Oct; 10:00–16:00, Nov–Mar, but opens 10:30 Wed and Fri throughout the year. In summer there are frequent classical concerts by the lake. For details of performances, tel: (020) 8348 1286.

**Above:** *Hampstead Heath is one of the most pleasant of London's parks by day. At night it's a noted pick-up area for gay men.*

## HIGHGATE

While not as prestigious as neighbouring Hampstead, Highgate has still had its share of famous residents (including Sir Francis Bacon and Samuel Coleridge), and can boast one of London's most famous graves, that of **Karl Marx**. Highgate (named after the country's oldest tollgate which once stood in the present-day High Street) is visited mainly for the extraordinary **Cemetery**, with its mausoleums, catacombs, and bizarre statuary. Others buried here include Christina Rossetti, Charles Dickens's wife Catherine, and author Mary Ann Evans (a.k.a. George Eliot).

The **West Cemetery** is the most interesting part, containing as it does numerous impressive vaults and statuary. Open 10:00–17:00 Monday–Friday, 11:00–17:00 Saturday and Sunday, Apr–Nov; 10:00–16:00 Monday–Friday, 11:00–16:00 Saturday and Sunday, Dec–Mar.

> **FAMOUS RESIDENTS**
>
> Almost every street in Hampstead seems to have blue plaques commemorating famous residents of the past: William Blake, Agatha Christie, Richard Burton, George Orwell, Robert Louis Stevenson, John Constable, Charles de Gaulle, John le Carré, Henry Moore, Peter Sellers, AA Milne, Edith Sitwell and Barbara Hepworth are just some of them. More recently, it has been home to celebrities such as Elizabeth Taylor, Sting, Boy George, Tom Conti, Emma Thompson, and Jeremy Irons, to name but a few. Hampstead's standing amongst the literati is well illustrated by the fact that actress Glenda Jackson was, until recently, the local Labour Party MP.

**Right:** *Colourful barges at Islington Lock on the Regent's Canal, a pleasant way to travel through parts of North London.*
**Opposite:** *St John's Gate (16th century) is one of the three medieval establishments that survive today.*

**INTERESTING WALKS**

Islington and Clerkwell are areas best explored on foot. Some 16 years ago local historian and lecturer Peter Powell began organizing and leading themed literary and historic strolls in the area. Now called **Angel Walks**, these cover such subjects as Joe Orton (a 1960s playwright with a lurid lifestyle and gruesome death), local pubs, Charles Dickens and the general area. Most leave at 10:30, so telephone in the afternoon: (020) 7226 8333.
For (mainly) afternoon walks, with themes such as country living, John Wesley, arts and crafts, and the domestic scene, contact the **Clerkenwell & Islington Guides Association**, tel: (020) 7622 3278.

## ISLINGTON

Islington was a spa resort that developed into a working class district. In the 1970s an influx of writers, media folk and left-leaning trendies led to today's lively mix of bistros, ethnic restaurants, quirky shops and unusual theatre venues. The **Almeida**, one of London's premier showcases for new talent, alternates classics and new plays. Unfortunately the renowned **King's Head Theatre Pub** is in desperate need of funding and its future is in doubt – as is that of the **Little Angel Puppet Theatre**.

Opposite Islington Green, the **Business Design Centre's** modern façade hides the Victorian brickwork of the old Royal Agricultural Hall (the 'Aggie'), one of the capital's earliest exhibition halls. The BDC keeps up the tradition, with a variety of fairs throughout the year. Further along Upper Street are the **Town Hall** and a gallery exhibiting works connected with Islington. For information, tel: (020) 7354 9442.

A short distance from Angel tube, on Pentonville Road, is a refurbished 19th-century chapel which is the headquarters of the **Crafts Council** and hosts changing crafts exhibitions; tel: (020) 7278 7700.

**Regent's Canal** emerges from a tunnel at the bottom of Duncan Street. Access to the towpath is from Colebrooke Row and it's possible to follow it all the way to Limehouse: with breaks at some interesting pubs along the way.

## Camden Passage **

Islington's main attraction is the **antiques market**, which is located just a few minutes' walk from Angel tube. It fills Camden Passage on Wednesday mornings and Saturdays, but the surrounding antique shops are open every day of the week. **Chapel Market** (open Tuesday to Saturday), on the other side of Upper Street, is a traditional London flea market.

## CLERKENWELL

Situated between Holborn and Islington, Clerkenwell has long been associated with craft industries and the opulent displays of **Hatton Garden** (off Holborn Circus), testify that it is still the main centre in the United Kingdom for the gemstone trade, while its other role as a centre of radical politics is reflected by the presence of the **Marx Memorial Library** on Clerkenwell Green. The library is open 13:00–18:00 Mon, 13:00–20:00 Tue–Thurs, 10:00–13:00 Sat.

## Museum of the Order of St John *

The crusading Knights Hospitallers were based here and the remains of their 13th-century priory are to the southeast of Clerkenwell Green. The most conspicuous remnant is **St John's Gate**, now containing a museum about the Order. Open 10:00–17:00, Mon–Fri; 10:00–16:00 Sat. To see the **Grand Priory crypt** and the rooms inside the **Gatehouse** and **Chapter Hall**, you must join a tour (11:00 and 14:30 Tue, Fri, Sat).

## Charterhouse *

A few minutes' walk from St John's Gate is Charterhouse, a 14th–17th-century Carthusian monastery (and later a private charity school). The complex includes monks' cells and Renaissance ornamentation in the Great Hall and Great Chamber. It can be visited only on tours: be at the gate at 14:15 on Wed, April–July.

---

**LITTLE ITALY**

In the 19th century Italian immigrants were in demand for their skills as painters, artisans and also dancing and fencing teachers. They established their own **Little Italy** in Clerkenwell around Rosebery Avenue, Farringdon Road and Clerkenwell Road. Its focal point was **St Peter's Italian Church** and though nowadays the 10,000 Italians who originally lived here have settled elsewhere, there are still Italian restaurants, delicatessens and wine merchants in the vicinity.

---

**MOUNT PLEASANT**

Post offices don't normally feature much as tourist attractions but the **Mount Pleasant Sorting Office** – the largest in the country – is unique in that it has its own private underground railway system which shuttles down a network of tunnels to other sorting offices, a miniature (and driverless) version of the tube. Viewing is by arrangement; tel: (020) 7239 2312.

# 8
# South of the Thames

London's traditional draws are mostly north of the Thames and many visitors are unaware of the riches to be found along the south bank. A pleasant walk, mostly beside the river, links them all; from Lambeth to Butler's Wharf.

The **South Bank Centre** has grown from the original (1950s) Festival of Britain site and is Europe's largest arts complex, with a selection of galleries, concert halls, cinemas and theatres – including the **Royal National Theatre** and **National Film Theatre** – and it's constantly expanding.

A little to the south, what was the old **County Hall** has recently developed into another entertainment centre: from the elegant **British Airways London Eye** (a giant ferris wheel) to the extraordinary **Dalí Universe** and superb **London Aquarium**. Further south, **Lambeth's** attractions include the excellent **Imperial War Museum** and a charming **Museum of Garden History**.

Heading in the other direction, you reach the offbeat shops and other attractions of the **Oxo Tower Wharf** and, beyond them, **Bankside**, where the vast new **Tate Modern** provides a complete contrast to the reconstruction of Shakespeare's **Globe Theatre**. Beyond Southwark Bridge, there's **Vinopolis** – a must for lovers of wine – and ancient **Southwark Cathedral**. Continuing east, the horrors of the ever-popular **London Dungeon** attract long queues, while *HMS Belfast* can easily accommodate hordes of visitors. The last stretch is **Butler's Wharf**, just east of Tower Bridge, where the interesting **Design Museum** and little **Tea and Coffee Museums** are located.

## DON'T MISS

**\*\*\* London Eye:** unrivalled views of the capital.
**\*\*\* Shakespeare's Globe:** authentic recreation of the original auditorium and a comprehensive exhibition.
**\*\*\* Tate Modern:** 20th-century art in all its forms.
**\*\*\* Thames boat to Greenwich:** home of several fascinating attractions.
**\*\* Vinopolis:** sample wines from all over the world.
**\*\* Imperial War Museum:** comprehensive coverage of modern warfare.
**\*\* London Aquarium:** all forms of marine life.

**Opposite:** *The Imperial War Museum has fascinating displays.*

## LAMBETH

### Imperial War Museum ★★

From the horrors of the trenches of Flanders to hi-tech battles of the Gulf War, modern warfare is presented in the Imperial War Museum. The main gallery features tanks, V2 rockets, a Spitfire and a Polaris missile. Interactive exhibits include walk-through World War I trenches (complete with mud, rats and simulated shellfire), a recreated Blitz scenario in the bomb-ravaged streets of wartime London, and the Secret War (about spies). The latest addition is the Holocaust Exhibition (get a timed ticket), a harrowing audiovisual depiction of the Nazi campaign against all undesirables, with inevitable concentration on the Jews, and including a scale model of Auschwitz. Open 10:00–18:00 daily.

### Florence Nightingale Museum ★

On a corner of St Thomas's Hospital, where the 'Lady with the Lamp' set up the first professional school of nursing, is a small museum devoted to the indefatigable

---

**LAMBETH PALACE**

As Westminster began to emerge as the focus for political and royal power in the 13th century, the clergy decided they had to have a presence nearby, so the Bishop of Winchester built **Southwark Palace** (of which little remains), and the then Archbishop of Canterbury built **Lambeth Palace**, which is still the Archbishop's London residence. This palace is seldom open to the public.

---

**NAMCOSTATION**

Also in County Hall, and likely to be popular with the younger members of the family, this is a mostly hi-tech entertainment centre with simulators and video games. It also offers pool tables, dodgems and ten-pin bowling. Open daily 10:00 till midnight.

---

**Right:** *The attractive Tudor Gatehouse at Lambeth Palace.*

campaigner, with audiovisual presentations and recreations of the Crimean military hospitals where she earned her reputation as a heroine. Open 10:00–16:00, Monday–Friday; 11:30–15:30, Saturday–Sunday.

## Museum of Garden History *

Next door to Lambeth Palace, inside a deconsecrated church are displays on the development of garden design and early plant hunters (such as 17th-century Royal Gardener, John Tradescant, who travelled widely to bring new species back to Britain). Outside, there is a period garden with, unexpectedly, the sarcophagus of Captain Bligh of *Mutiny on the Bounty* fame. Open 10:30–17:00 daily, March–November.

## COUNTY HALL
### London Aquarium **

Suitably positioned beside the Thames, in County Hall, the Aquarium is on two levels. Do not take the escalator up from the lower level until you are ready to leave: there is no way back. The place is split into geographical areas and tanks recreate all the different watery habitats to be found on earth, ranging from freshwater streams to the ocean depths. Highlights include a peaceful tank of small jellyfish, an enormous shark tank and a touch tank with friendly rays. Open 10:00–17:00 daily (19:00 during school holidays).

---

**FROG TOURS**

Based at County Hall (bookings on the river side – or tel: (020) 7928 3132; departures on the other side, from Belvedere Road), Frog Tours offer amphibious vehicles: a definitely unusual way of seeing the City of Westminster. The full tour (with commentary) lasts about an hour and a half, roughly a third of it actually on the Thames. Departs daily every 30 minutes from 10:00 to dusk.

---

**BFI FILM CENTRE**

This innovative new centre devoted to the world of film is due to open in 2003/2004. It will be situated underneath a raised area of the newly landscaped Jubilee Gardens: now being created to fill the area between the London Eye and the Royal Festival Hall. Among other things, the new complex will incorporate a reference library and an enlarged National Film Theatre. The highlight will undoubtedly be the revamped **Museum of the Moving Image (MOMI)** – this was a 'must' for film buffs even in its original form, covering everything from the earliest cameras to the latest Hollywood blockbusters, and we are promised that the new version will be bigger and better, with even more interactive exhibits.

---

**Left:** *The Royal Festival Hall is located at the South Bank Centre.*

**Above:** *The aptly named London Eye provides an overview of the capital.*
**Opposite:** *The Globe Theatre, where Shakespeare's plays are performed as in the 1600s.*

### Dalí Universe ★★

This new museum inside County Hall (entrance on the river side) has a collection of bizarre paintings, sculptures, graphics, jewellery and furniture created by the eccentric Spanish Surrealist: a must for aficionados and fascinating for non-fans. Open daily 10:00–17:30.

### British Airways London Eye ★★★

A new addition to the London skyline, visible for miles, the Eye is the world's largest observation wheel. It soars 135m (450ft) above the Thames, the glass capsules providing unrivalled all-round views. 'Flights' last about 30 minutes, 09:00–21:30, April to mid-September; 10:00–17:30, mid-September to March. Bookings in person at County Hall or by phone, tel: (0870) 500 0600 (at least two days in advance, and have your credit card number handy – it's a recorded service).

### THE SOUTH BANK
### South Bank Centre ★★

Across the Thames from the Savoy, the vast range of arts, music, drama, film and poetry events staged within the South Bank Centre make it one of the main cultural hubs of the city. The centre developed after the 1951 Festival of Britain, a postwar effort to boost morale, with the South Bank Exhibition as its centrepiece.

The oldest building in the complex is the **Royal Festival Hall** (RFH), built in 1951 with a sound-proofed auditorium suspended above the foyer. The RFH is one of the capital's main concert venues, with the London Philharmonic as its resident orchestra. Jazz, dance and ballet are also staged here. The other main concert halls are the **Queen Elizabeth Hall** and the more intimate **Purcell Room**. Behind these venues is the **Hayward Gallery** (open daily 10:00–18:00, closing 20:00 Tue–Wed), easily located by the tall neon sculpture on its roof. The

Hayward hosts major classical and contemporary art exhibitions. Downstream, the **Royal National Theatre** contains three auditoriums (the Olivier, Lyttelton and Cottesloe theatres), which stage a wide variety of productions, and there are various al fresco events on the forecourt. Then there is the **National Film Theatre** (NFT), which has three auditoriums where over 2000 films are screened each year, and talks, workshops and lectures are hosted. The London Film Festival is held here every November. The NFT is likely to move temporarily to the West End, pending completion of the new BFI Film Centre (*see* box, p. 95). Film fans can still visit the **BFI Imax Cinema**, which boasts the largest screen in Britain: the height of a ten-storey building! There is a repertoire of half a dozen films, some 3D, so something to suit most tastes. For details, tel: (020) 7902 1234.

### Shakespeare's Globe Exhibition ★★★
The Globe Theatre is a faithful recreation of the original structure of the early 1600s – the first thatched building in the capital since the Great Fire of London. In summer (May–Sept), Shakespeare's works are presented as they would have been in his day (apart from the fact that there are now actresses). The techniques are best appreciated if you take the tour before attending a performance. A permanent exhibition, *All the World's a Stage*, uses a combination of modern technology and traditional skills to cover Bankside, Shakespeare, his theatres, actors and audiences. A tour of the actual theatre is included. Open daily 10:00–17:00, Oct–April; 09:00–12:00, May–Sept.

### Tate Modern ★★★
Once an ugly power station, London's latest gallery is now a stunning architectural mix of new and old, with stupendous views from the

| | |
|---|---|
| **THE GLOBE THEATRE** | |

Shakespeare's plays were written for his theatre on the banks of the Thames, known as the 'Wooden O', and it was here that *King Lear*, *Macbeth*, *Hamlet*, *Othello* and many other productions were first staged. It was closed down by the Puritans in 1642. The current recreation is largely due to the American film-maker Sam Wanamaker, who came to London in 1949 expecting to find a Globe Theatre and, disappointed, set about raising funds to rebuild it; he died in 1993, but his vision has finally been realized. A full performance season in the half-covered theatre (which holds an audience of 1500) began in 1997.

| | |
|---|---|
| **GABRIEL'S WHARF** | |

This is a pleasant little enclave full of eateries and craft shops: you can often watch such things as jewellery and ceramics being created.

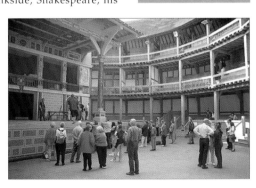

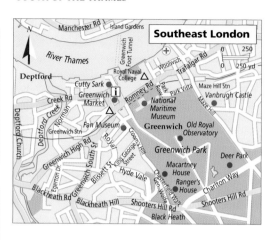

**Southeast London**

---

### SKYLINE BALLOON

For a different perspective, try a ride in a tethered balloon: a 15-minute ascent from just be-side Tower Bridge takes you up to 400m in perfect weather – but it's grounded when windy, so check, tel: (020) 7378 8252. When conditions are right, the flights are daily 09:00–22:00.

---

### *GOLDEN HINDE*

Moored in Clink Street is a full-size reconstruction of Sir Francis Drake's 16th-century warship, *Golden Hinde*, complete with costumed crew. Open daily, but times vary; tel: (0870) 011 8700.

---

### MILLENNIUM BRIDGE

Since Tower Bridge (in 1894), central London had had no new Thames bridge and it was felt that a pedestrian crossing linking Bankside with the City of London would be a way to celebrate the new century, so the innovative Millennium Bridge was opened in May 2000. Unfortunately the crowd that thronged onto it caused it to sway, frightening many people and raising doubts (probably unfounded) about its safety. It closed after only a few days and is unlikely to re-open until some method has been devised to make it more stable. In the meantime, the elegant structure is best viewed from the upper levels of Tate Modern.

---

7th-floor café. Much of the Tate Gallery's enormous collection has been languishing unseen for decades, due to lack of space. Now, at last, hundreds of paintings and sculptures are once again on view. Arranged by subject, rather than style or chronology, there are four themed galleries which enable viewers to appreciate the changing styles of the 20th century. Films and televisions are scattered through the building to lend an extra dimension and long-established favourites (such as Monet's *Water Lilies* and Rodin's *The Kiss*) mingle with controversial works that many people consider to be totally devoid of artistic merit (such as the infamous bricks). Open daily 10:15–17:50, Sun–Thurs; 10:15–22:00, Fri.

## SOUTHWARK
### Southwark Cathedral ★★
Although it has been a cathedral only since 1905, the building is rich in history, having grown from a 13th-century church which incorporated part of the floor of a Roman villa and featured artefacts from many centuries. Now extensive excavations and multi-media presentations are being prepared for public consumption and late 2000/early 2001 should see the cathedral become a major 21st-century attraction. Open daily 08:00–18:00, but restricted to worshippers during services.

## Vinopolis ★★

Not to be missed by wine lovers, Vinopolis (Bank End/Clink Street: signposted from the riverside) is devoted to the wines of the world, with audio tours of regions and their history. You can travel through the themed areas at your own pace and the entry fee includes five tastings (there are 200 wines from 16 countries from which to choose and you can buy extra tastings). Entry 10:00–15:30, Tuesday–Friday; 10:00–19:00, Monday; 10:00–18:00 Sunday. An art gallery, wine shop and excellent restaurant are also on offer.

## The Clink Prison ★★

Clink Prison is a small but atmospheric recreation in what remains of a real 12th-century prison, which has given its name as a slang term for all prisons. Open daily 10:00–21:00, May–September; 10:00–18:00, October–April.

## POOL OF LONDON
### HMS Belfast ★★

The largest surviving battle cruiser from World War II, *HMS Belfast* remained in service until 1965 and is now a floating museum, moored just upstream from Tower Bridge. This complex warship (which carried 800 crew) has nine decks and you can explore all of it, from the bridge down to the engine and boiler rooms. Open daily 10:00–16:00 Mar–Oct; 10:00–15:00 Nov–Feb.

## The London Dungeon ★★

Housed in vaults on Tooley Street, the dungeon is a macabre look at the gruesome aspects of history, with life-size tableaux (some animatronic) of people being beheaded, drawn and quartered, hanged, etc.

---

### HAY'S GALLERIA

Between London Bridge station and the river, **Hay's Galleria** is an unusual shopping precinct built over the former Hay's Dock with a curved glass-and-steel roof enclosing the warehouses on either side. It contains continental-style shops, bars and restaurants.

---

### SOUTHWARK INFORMATION CENTRE

At 6 Tooley Street, this centre has information covering the whole area. Open 10:00–18:00, Mon–Sat; 11:00–18:00 Sun; tel: (020) 7403 8299.

---

**Below:** *The London Dungeon offers London's most grisly entertainment and attracts vast crowds.*

**Opposite:** *Wren's Royal Naval College buildings at Greenwich, now open to the public, except when there are special functions.* **Below:** *Greenwich Park, looking down on the Queen's House.*

It ends with a boat ride through Traitor's Gate, leading to a tour of Jack the Ripper's London and a recreation of the Great Fire of London. Open daily 10:00–17:30, Apr–Sept; 10:00–16:30, Oct–Mar. Immensely popular, so be prepared to queue for some time.

### Britain at War Experience ★★
Just along from the London Dungeon, this evocative theme museum conveys the atmosphere of wartime London and how people coped during the Blitz (rationing, blackouts and so forth). It starts with a creaking elevator ride into an air-raid shelter and ends with an impressively realistic mock-up of a bombed-out, rubble-strewn street, complete with special effects such as smells and smoke. Open daily 10:00–17:30, Apr–Sept; 20:00–16:30, Oct–Mar.

### BUTLER'S WHARF
### Design Museum ★★
This museum, at Butler's Wharf, provides a revealing insight into design as it relates to everyday objects such as cars and furniture. There are both permanent and temporary exhibitions and displays include some products not yet in production. For details, tel: (020) 7940 8790. Open 11:30–17:30, Mon–Fri; 10:30–17:30, Sat–Sun.

### Bramah Tea and Coffee Museums ★
In Maguire Street, just back from the Design Museum, is a little museum with some thousand teapots and other items relating to England's favourite beverage. After admiring pots shaped as dragons and the like, you can sample the brew of your choice and home-made cakes in the small café. The even smaller Coffee Museum is just round the corner: ask for it to be opened (no extra charge). Open daily 10:00–18:00.

## GREENWICH

One of London's most attractive villages, Greenwich makes a pleasant excursion along the Thames, where 16 galleries cover everything ranging from Viking ships to the *Titanic*.

### National Maritime Museum ★★★

Britain's seafaring history (from the 15th century to the Falklands War) is the main theme of this museum. One of the focal points is a gallery featuring **20th Century Sea Power** but one of the most exciting exhibits is the **Nelson Gallery**, which brings together material on the private and public lives of Admiral Lord Nelson – including the coat he was wearing at the Battle of Trafalgar (with the hole made by the musket ball which killed him, and the ball itself – salvaged by the ship's surgeon – alongside). Turner's *Victory of the Battle of Trafalgar* is a highlight, with a taped commentary and simulation of the battle. In the interactive **All Hands** gallery you can try out seafaring skills. Open 10:00–16:30 daily.

### The Queen's House

The beautiful features of this historic building, designed by Inigo Jones, are now obscured by a series of exhibitions (due to continue until 2003), but complaints have been numerous and it is possible that public pressure will result in the house being restored to its former glory.

---

**FAN MUSEUM**

This delightful little specialist museum, a few minutes' walk from the pier, at 12 Crooms Hill, has changing themed exhibitions formed by displaying a few dozen unusual fans from a collection of over 2000. Open 11:00–16:30, Tue–Sat; 12:00–16:30 Sun.

---

**TIME IN GREENWICH**

During the early 19th century most parts of Britain ran on different time zones. This was fine during the days of stage-coach travel, but it made the timetables of the newly emerging rail network particularly confusing. From 1852 London time was adopted as standard, but clocks still showed both local and London time; this continued until 1884 when Greenwich Mean Time (GMT) was adopted as the standard by which not just Britain but the whole world set its clocks. An international convention placed Longitude 0 degs (the imaginary line joining the North and South Poles) at Greenwich, and by standing on this Meridian (an illuminated line on the ground) at the Old Royal Observatory you are straddling the eastern and western hemispheres. The red time ball on top of Flamsteed House (the old observatory) is raised and dropped every day – as it has been for over a century – at 13:00 as a time signal to shipping on the River Thames.

**EXPLORING GREENWICH**

The easiest way to reach Greenwich is by boat or by taking the Docklands Light Railway (DLR) to Cutty Sark station. Greenwich Royal Park, once the private hunting ground of royalty, is a lovely area to wander around. There are daily guided walks at 12:15 and 14:15, starting at the **Tourist Information Centre**, to the starboard (right) side of *Cutty Sark*. The very helpful centre is open daily 10:00–17:00 (often later in summer), tel: (020) 8858 6376. There is an excellent weekend arts and crafts market: tel: (020) 7515 7153 for details.

### The Old Royal Naval College ★★

Highlights of Wren's Royal Naval College are the magnificent **Painted Hall**, with decorations that took nearly 20 years to complete, and the elegant **Chapel**, where concerts and recitals are regularly performed. Open 10:00–16:15, Mon–Sat; 12:30–16:15 Sun.

### The Old Royal Observatory ★★

Built in 1676 for Charles II's Royal Astronomer, the Old Royal Observatory sits atop the hill (there's a shuttle bus every 15 minutes) in Greenwich Park on the Greenwich Meridian line, and has an interesting display on time and astronomy, with old telescopes and other instruments. One of the exhibits is the first marine chronometer, probably 'the most important timepiece ever made' since it enabled ships to calculate longitude, and so navigate accurately for the first time. Open 10:00–16:30 daily. There's a stunning view over Greenwich Park and Queen Anne's House to Canary Wharf, with *Cutty Sark*'s rigging to the left and the **Millennium Dome** to the right.

### *Cutty Sark* and *Gypsy Moth IV* ★★

On board the *Cutty Sark* are the original gilded teak fittings, the rigging on its three masts, and a lot of maritime memorabilia. The below-decks area houses colourful figureheads, and some cabins above contain tableaux of what ship life was like. Built on the Clyde in 1869, the *Cutty Sark* was one of the last tea clippers, fast sailing ships which competed each year to bring the first of the new tea crop back from China. Open 10:00–16:30 daily.

*Gypsy Moth IV* looks tiny alongside the *Cutty Sark*'s 50m (164ft) masts. This 16m (52ft) ketch was the first to be sailed around the world single-handed, when Francis Chichester made his record-breaking circum-navigation in 1966–1967. On his return, he was knighted by Her Majesty the Queen with Sir Francis Drake's sword. *Gypsy Moth IV* can't be boarded and there are rumours that she may be purchased for a museum.

## WOOLWICH
### The Thames Barrier *

London has always lived with the threat of flooding from the Thames, an event which occurs far more frequently than might be expected. A flood barrier was first pro-posed in the 19th century, but it wasn't until the 1980s that one was actually built – a unique and impressive structure it is too, with its ten massive stainless steel gates, each weighing 3700 tonnes, which take half-an-hour to be raised or lowered. They have been used to prevent floods more than 20 times since being completed, and are tested every month. For schedules, tel: (020) 8305 4188.

There are good views of the structure – the largest movable flood barrier in the world – from the visitors centre, which has information on their construction and operation. Open 10:00–17:00, Monday–Friday; 10:30–17:30 weekends. For a clear view of the barrier from the river, take a boat trip from Greenwich.

### Woolwich Railway Museum *

The Railway Museum, Pier Road, is a must for all railway enthusiasts. It is located at the old Railway Station and depicts the history of the Great Eastern Railway, founded in 1862, and includes some restored steam engines. Open 13:00–17:00, Sat–Sun all year; also Mon, Tue and Wed during school holidays. To check, tel: (020) 7474 7244.

**Above:** *The Thames Barrier at Woolwich.*
**Opposite:** *The Royal Observatory at Greenwich has set the standard for global time for over three centuries.*

---

**MILITARY WOOLWICH**

Woolwich has a long history as a military depot, starting with the creation of the **Royal Dockyards** in 1513 by Henry VIII. Both Sir Walter Raleigh and Captain Cook set out on their historic voyages of discovery from the docks here, which eventually closed in 1869. The buildings of the **Royal Arsenal** (where gun-powder was manufactured in the 17th century) are undergoing a £25 million conversion into **Firepower!** – a Royal Artillery Museum – due to open in May 2001.

# 9
# Nearby Excursions

There are many interesting places to visit just a short distance from the centre of London. **Chiswick**, in West London, is a quaint village-like area, with riverside pubs – such as the City Barge at Strand-on-the-Green, dating from 1484, and reached from Kew Bridge (near the Steam Museum) – and the splendours of **Chiswick House** all within easy walking distance.

As the River Thames loops its way southwards, it passes through **Kew** and **Richmond**, affluent suburbs which have enjoyed Royal patronage from the 12th century, when palaces were built here on the riverbanks. The fabulous **Kew Gardens** is one of the chief legacies of the old royal estates, as is the walled **Richmond Park**, where herds of deer roam among the bracken and coppices. Other attractions include stately mansions such as **Syon House** and **Osterley House**.

Still further to the southwest is **Hampton Court**, one of the greatest of the Royal palaces, with wonderfully opulent rooms hidden away behind its red-brick exterior. The magnificent gardens add to the allure of this vast palace, which is well worth the 20km (12½ mile) journey out from the centre of town.

And, of course, no visit to London would be complete without a trip to **Windsor Castle**, although it is some 40km (25 miles) from the city centre. A palpable sense of nearly a thousand years of history pervades this towered and turreted complex on a hilltop above the Thames. You can tour the royal apartments and view some of the superb Royal Collection.

### DON'T MISS

**\*\*\* Hampton Court Palace** and **Windsor Castle:** royal residences filled with history.
**\*\*\* Kew Gardens:** visit the lush Palm House as well as the Temperate House.
**\*\*\* Wetland Centre, Barnes:** wonderful new habitat for waterfowl (see p. 8).
**\*\* Syon** and **Osterley House:** lordly riverbank mansions.
**\*\* Richmond Park:** vast royal hunting grounds.
**\* Chiswick:** traditional pub lunches, overlooking the Thames riverside.

**Opposite:** *Henry VIII's magnificent Tudor palace at Hampton Court.*

ON FOOT TO CHISWICK

There is an enjoyable **riverside walkway** between Hammersmith and Chiswick, starting just underneath Hammersmith Bridge and continuing along the Thames all the way to Chiswick Mall and the village centre. Along the way there are several popular riverside **pubs** with houseboats moored alongside, amongst them the historic Dove (dating from the 17th century; in later years literary figures such as Ernest Hemingway, William Morris and Graham Greene all frequented it) as well as others such as the Black Lion, the Old Ship Inn, the Rutland and the Blue Anchor. All these riverside pubs are packed to overflowing with spectators during the annual Oxford/Cambridge boat race.

**Below:** *Walpole House at Chiswick. Its riverside village atmosphere, pubs and architecture make Chiswick an enjoyable excursion choice.*

## CHISWICK

Its pleasant riverside location makes the village of Chiswick a good finishing point for a walk along the banks of the Thames, with the attractive **Chiswick Mall** boasting a series of grand houses overlooking the houseboats moored on the tidal reaches. The atmospheric **Church Lane** was the original medieval high street, with the graveyard of the church of **St Nicholas** (which has a 15th-century tower) containing the graves of painters JM Whistler and William Hogarth. **Hogarth's House** is just a short stroll away, with many of his famous satirical engravings – which so enraged the establishment at the time – displayed inside. Open 13:00–17:00, Tuesday–Friday (16:00 Nov–Mar); 13:00–18:00, Saturday–Sunday (17:00 Nov–Mar).

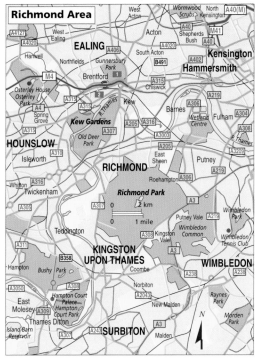

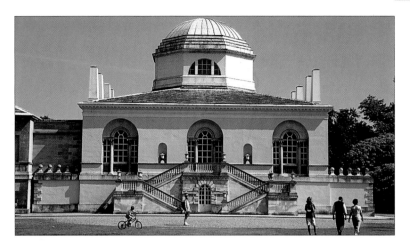

## Chiswick House ★★

The highlight of Chiswick is undoubtedly Chiswick House, a classical, Palladian-style villa built by arts patron Lord Burlington in 1729. It was designed as a gallery for his art collection and as a setting for meeting his coterie, which included leading intellectuals of the time such as Alexander Pope and Jonathan Swift, and composers such as Handel. The inside of the house has a special domed octagonal hall at its centre, where paintings and sculptures were once displayed. Don't miss the sumptuously re-decorated Blue Velvet Room or the noted Chiswick Tables (in the gallery). The house is surrounded by superb gardens, complete with Roman statuary and an Ionic temple overlooking a grassy amphitheatre with a pond at its centre. Open 10:00–17:30, Apr–Sept; 10:00–16:30, Oct; 10:00–15:30, Wed–Sun, Nov–Mar.

## Kew Bridge Steam Museum ★

This old Victorian water works features a massive Steam Hall with four monster Cornish beam engines, maintained by volunteers and fired up at weekends – which is evidently the best time to visit if you're a steam enthusiast. There's also a miniature steam railway and displays on the history of water power. Open 11:00–17:00, daily.

**Above:** *Built around a central octagonal room, Chiswick House is a classic example of Palladian-style architecture.*
**Below:** *Chiswick Mall and Church, seen from the Thames.*

**Right:** *Osterley House, a fine example of neoclassical Robert Adam architecture.*
**Opposite:** *Victoria Regis water lilies in the Princess of Wales Conservatory at Kew Gardens.*

## SYON AND OSTERLEY

### Syon House **

One of several mansions renovated by the talented designer Robert Adam in the late 1700s, Syon contains one of London's most exuberant period interiors, notably the splendid Great Hall. The walls of the Long Gallery are hung with Old Masters. House open 11:00–17:00, Wed–Sun and holiday Mon, Mar/Apr–Oct. The grounds were designed by Capability Brown and are open daily all year 10:00–17:30 – or dusk, if earlier. They encompass a trout fishery, garden centre, organic produce shop, **Butterfly House**, full of free-flying butterflies (open 10:00–17:00 daily, but till 15:30 in winter) and **Aquatic Experience**, which protects species of fish, birds, reptiles and mammals endangered in the wild (open 10:00–18:00 daily, but till 17:00 in winter).

### Osterley House and Park *

One of the last great country houses with an intact estate within the London area, Osterley House is approached through the park along an avenue of towering chestnut trees, and past an ornamental lake with a pagoda. The neoclassical house is one of the finest remaining examples of the work of Robert Adam and has richly decorated interiors. The house is open 13:00–16:30, Wed–Sun, Apr–Oct. The Park is open year-round from 09:00 to sunset daily.

---

**FLOWERING SEASONS AT KEW**

- **January:** Camellias, shrubs, alpines and heathers.
- **February:** Crocuses and snowdrops.
- **March:** Daffodils and cherry blossom.
- **April:** Magnolias, tulips and spring bedding.
- **May:** Bluebells, azaleas and lilac.
- **June:** Roses, rhododendrons and chestnut trees.
- **July & August:** Giant waterlily, summer bedding and scented plants.
- **September:** Summer bulbs and start of autumn colour.
- **October:** Late-flowering crocuses and cyclamens.
- **November:** The last of the autumn foliage.
- **December:** Strawberry trees and holly.

# Kew

## Kew Gardens ★★★

Covering 121ha (300 acres) on the banks of the Thames between Richmond and Kew, the Royal Botanic Gardens is a fascinating place to visit. It houses one of the greatest collections of plants and plant material in the world, and is a major research centre for the economic and medicinal uses of plants. Kew Gardens also boasts four of the largest glasshouses in the world.

The main entrance to the Gardens (open 09:30 till dusk, daily) is on Lichfield Road at the Victoria Gate, where you should pick up a map at the Visitor Centre before setting off to explore the Gardens. Almost directly opposite is the magnificent **Palm House**, a masterpiece of Victorian engineering in iron and glass. Nearby is the **Waterlily House**, Kew's most humid environment, where sacred lotus bloom in summer. To the west of here is the elegant **Temperate House**, the largest of Kew's glasshouses and a superb setting for many exotic species, citrus fruits, and the world's largest indoor plant (the Chilean Wine Palm). The new **Evolution House**, behind it, traces the development of plant life on the planet over the last 3500 million years.

Other highlights – of which there are many – within the gardens include a towering **Pagoda**, the **Marianne North Gallery** (which houses 832 botanical paintings by this talented Victorian artist), **Queen Charlotte's Cottage** (once a royal summer house), and the **Princess of Wales Conservatory** for tropical plants. The smallest royal residence in the country is the intimate **Kew Palace**, tucked away on the north side of the gardens; George III and Queen Charlotte used it as their family retreat from 1802–1818. Due to re-open in 2001, after major restoration.

**Right:** *A view of the Thames from Richmond. Easily accessible from the city centre, Richmond, with its famous park, beautiful buildings and riverside location, has a great deal to offer visitors.*
**Opposite:** *Riverboats at Hampton Court.*

## RICHMOND

This riverside town's main attraction is its enormous Park (*see below*), but there are other sights nearby which are of interest. Between the modern high street and the Thames lies **Richmond Green**, a lovely square surrounded by Queen Anne and Georgian houses. On the southwest corner a Tudor gateway is all that remains of **Richmond Palace**, dating back to the 12th century but extensively rebuilt by the Tudors. A famous view, embracing the Thames Valley and no less than six counties, is the main reward for climbing **Richmond Hill** behind the town.

### Richmond Park ★★

Beyond Richmond Hill stretches the huge expanse of Richmond Park, created by Charles I who hunted here and enclosed it within a 16km (10 mile) long wall (still there today) in the 17th century. At 1000ha (2471 acres) it is easily the largest city park in Europe, and features rolling grasslands interspersed with coppices, woodland (mostly oak, beech and chestnut) and ponds. Much of this is natural wilderness, apart from the landscaped plantations of rhododendron and azaleas, which provide gorgeous displays in the spring. Sizeable herds of red and fallow deer roam all over the park, and twitchers will also find plenty of birdlife (particularly in **Sidmouth Wood**, which is a bird sanctuary).

## HAMPTON COURT PALACE

Set in 24ha (59 acres) of landscaped gardens and park-lands on the banks of the River Thames, Hampton Court is probably the most dazzling of all the royal palaces in England. Don't forget to try the renowned maze. Of all the monarchs who have lived here it is most closely associated with Henry VIII, and today the tapestry of court life in Tudor times is vividly brought to life by costumed actors leading tours through this rambling, turreted building.

Entering the **palace** you should first explore the three **courtyards**, namely the Base Court, the Clock Court, and the Fountain Court.

Retrace your steps to the Base Court and **Henry VIII's State Apartments**, where the Great Hall has an ornate double-hammerbeam roof – Shakespeare's theatrical players performed here under Elizabeth I. Other major rooms include the Great Watching Chamber, the Haunted Gallery, and the Royal Chapel. Within the **Queen's Apartments** the most impressive room is probably the Queen's Drawing Room. Within the **King's Apartments** (built for William III), don't miss the vast display of armoury in the King's Guard Chamber. The prodigious consumption of the Royal Court is vividly brought to life in the massive **Tudor Kitchens**, which have been restored to show preparations for a feast day in 1542. Open 10:15–17:15 Monday; 09:30–17:15, Tuesday–Sunday, March–October; 10:15–15:45 Monday, 09:30–15:45, Tuesday–Sunday, October–March.

# WINDSOR

**Below:** *Guardsmen outside St George's Chapel, Windsor Castle.*

The network of cobbled streets of Windsor's Old Town is filled with antique and souvenir shops and features several interesting buildings, including **Burford House** (where Charles II housed his mistress Nell Gwynne), and the **Guildhall,** standing on pillars in the High Street, which was completed by Sir Christopher Wren.

## Windsor Castle ***

The oldest and largest inhabited castle in England and the official weekend residence of the Queen, Windsor Castle's imposing battlements and turrets dominate the town from its hilltop site, 40km (25 miles) from central London.

Originally a timber and earth stronghold built by William the Conqueror, the castle steadily grew in importance during Norman and Plantagenet times and was rebuilt in stone by Henry II. The present design of the castle was influenced by George III and his son, George IV, and it was the latter that added a bigger **Round Tower** – one of the castle's most distinguishing features – and many of the state apartments.

Entering the castle you go through the Middle Ward, with the Round Tower in its centre. Continue past the Winchester Gates to the North Terrace, where there are superb views over the Chiltern Hills and Eton College. Here is the entrance to the **State Apartments**, badly damaged in a major fire in 1992 but now fully restored to their former splendour. Amid the gilded ceilings and ornate furnishings are several important works by Rubens, Rembrandt and Van Dyck as well as superb Gobelin tapestries. Don't miss the exquisite **Queen Mary's Dolls House**, an extraordinary creation which took three years to complete. Designed by Edwin Lutyens in 1920, the house has working plumbing, lifts, and electricity. Nearby is the **Gallery**, which features themed exhibitions from the extensive Royal Collection of paintings, sculpture and objets d'art. Open 09:45–16:00 daily, March–October; 09:45–15:00 daily, November–February.

Passing through the Lower Ward you reach **St George's Chapel**, one of the finest ecclesiastical buildings in England, begun in 1475 by Edward IV. Ten monarchs (including Henry VIII and his favourite wife, Jane Seymour) are buried here; one of the best times to visit the chapel is when the choir is singing evensong (17:15 daily).

**GETTING THERE**

Windsor is around 45 minutes by train from central London, with frequent services from Waterloo to Windsor Riverside and from Paddington to Windsor Central (change at Slough). Both stations are close to the town centre. For details on train times or other information contact the Information Centre, 24 High Street, tel: (01753) 743 900. Open daily 09:30–18:00, July–Aug; 10:00–17:30 June; 10:00–17:00, Apr–May, Sept and early Oct; 10:00–16:00, mid-Oct–Mar.

**Overleaf:** *The dome of St Paul's, dominating the City skyline by night.*
**Below:** *Windsor Castle viewed from the Long Walk.*

## Eton *

A short walk takes you from Windsor to Eton, home of one of Britain's most famous 'public' schools, where pupils wear a characteristic uniform of top hat and morning coat. Over the years, Eton has educated many of the country's prime ministers and top politicians.

# London at a Glance

London's unpredictable weather (see p. 7) means that it is always best to pack an umbrella and raincoat. Despite seasonal fluctuations, the city's climate is essentially temperate and there may be sunny days almost throughout the year. **October–April** are probably the least crowded, with the peak (long queues at major attractions) July–August. Many prices are the same year-round, but book summer accommodation well in advance.

## GETTING THERE

**By Air:** There are direct flights to the UK from all major cities. The main airports for international flights are **Heathrow**, **Gatwick** and **Stansted**.
• **Heathrow:** 24km (14 miles) west of central London. The fastest way to the city centre is by Heathrow Express into Paddington, which takes 15 minutes and runs every 15 minutes from 05:00–23:40. The **Piccadilly Underground Line** is cheaper, takes 30–50 minutes and runs every 4 to 7 minutes 05:30–00:30, Mon–Sat, 07:30–23:30 Sun. The **Airbus** takes an hour. Route A1 takes you to Victoria via Earl's Court and Kensington. Route A2 goes to King's Cross via Bayswater and Bloomsbury. **Taxis** from Heathrow are expensive (allow £40).
• **Gatwick:** 50km (30 miles) south of London. The **Gatwick Express** runs from

the airport to Victoria Station (30 minutes), departing every 15 minutes 05:20–23:45 (hourly 00:30–04:30).
• **Stansted:** 60km (37 miles) northeast is London's newest airport. **Stansted Express** runs to Liverpool Street station (45 min), departing every half-hour, 05:00–23:00.
• **London City Airport:** In London Docklands, mostly used by commuters to and from Paris, Brussels, Amsterdam and other European cities. **Shuttle bus** to Liverpool Street Station (30 min) every 10 minutes, or to connect with the **Docklands Light Railway**, Canary Wharf.

**By Road and Sea:** Visitors from Europe may choose **ferry services** from the Channel ports or the **Channel Tunnel**. Services through the tunnel include **Le Shuttle** for drivers and **Eurostar** trains for passengers running direct from Paris and Brussels with connecting services from other European departure points.

## GETTING AROUND

London has an extensive public transport system: red double-decker **buses** (many are now seen in different liveries), **black taxis**, and the **Underground** trains (the 'tube'). Congested streets mean that the tube remains the quickest and most practical mode of travel.
**The Underground:** There are 12 lines, covering most districts but sparse south of the Thames.

Trains run 05:30–00:30. (07:30–23:30 Sundays); tickets available from machines or booths. The tube operates on a zone system, with a standard fare for all stations within a zone: the more zones you cross the more expensive the ticket will be. Travellers without tickets face fines of £10.
**Buses:** Travelling by **bus** has the bonus of sightseeing from the top deck. Most buses run 06:00–24:00; **night buses** (N prefix before the route number) run 24:00–06:00. There are two types of bus stop: compulsory ones (the sign has a white background) and request stops (with a red background). It's a flat rate of £1 for any central bus journey. On most buses you pay the driver on entry, but on some older Routemaster buses (with an open rear platform) a conductor will collect fares.
**Taxis:** London's famous **black cabs** (nowadays often coloured or covered in sponsors' adverts) run on meters according to the distance travelled and time of day. Taxis can be hailed on the street (when the yellow TAXI sign is lit, it means they are available). Radio Taxis tel: (020) 7272 0272. Computer Cabs (020) 7286 0286. **Mini cabs** are cheaper but the driver's street knowledge is less professional; always agree a price before setting off. They are not allowed to pick up passengers in the street.

# London at a Glance

## The West End
### LUXURY
**Brown's Hotel**, 30–34 Albemarle Street, W1, tel: (020) 7493 6020. Popular, old-fashioned; furnished with antiques, refurbished 1995.
**Claridge's**, Brook Street, W1, tel: (020) 7629 8860. Favourite with royalty and superstars. It's expensive, but service is good.
**The Dorchester**, 53 Park Lane, W1, tel: (020) 7629 8888. One of London's landmark hotels, overlooking Hyde Park, popular with movie stars.
**The London Hilton**, 22 Park Lane, W1, tel: (020) 7493 8000. Excellent views of Hyde Park; impeccable service and décor.
**The Ritz**, 150 Piccadilly, W1 tel: (020) 7493 8181. Steeped in history and an attraction in its own right, it has opulent Louis XVI décor with the west-facing rooms (facing Green Park) the best ones to book.

### MID-RANGE
**The Goring**, 15 Beeston Place, SW1, tel: (020) 7396 9000. Well-located, family-run hotel with elegant public rooms and spacious en-suite bedrooms.
**Hazlitt's**, 6 Frith Street, W1, tel: (020) 7434 1771. Period-style rooms in 18th-century home of essayist William Hazlitt.

## Bloomsbury and Covent Garden
### LUXURY
**The Savoy**, Strand, WC2, tel: (020) 7836 4343. Synonymous with top service and luxury; spacious rooms decorated in Art Deco. Good fitness centre.

### MID-RANGE
**Radisson Edwardian Mountbatten**, 20 Monmouth St, WC2, tel: (020) 7836 4300. Country-house-style hotel in Covent Garden, with Lord Mountbatten memorabilia.

### BUDGET
**Ruskin**, 23–24 Montague Street, WC1, tel: (020) 7636 7388. Excellent location in Bloomsbury, good value.

## West and Southwest London
### LUXURY
**Blakes**, 33 Roland Gardens, SW7, tel: (020) 7370 6701. Popular with celebrities. Glamorous interiors and suites.
**The Beaufort**, 33 Beaufort Gardens, SW3, tel: (020) 7584 5252. Stylish hotel with large, modern rooms and good value for money.

### MID-RANGE
**The Gallery Hotel**, 8–10 Queensberry Place, SW7, tel: (020) 7915 0000. Traditional Georgian with spacious suites.
**The Pelham**, 15 Cromwell Place, SW7, tel: (020) 7589 8288. Small, comfortable; with individually decorated rooms.

### BUDGET
**Amsterdam Hotel**, 7 Trebovir Road, SW5. Tel: (020) 7370 5084. Comfortable B&B near Earl's Court, all rooms with en-suite facilities.
**Hotel 167**, 167 Old Brompton Rd, SW5, tel: (020) 7373 0672. Slightly upmarket B&B, all rooms with en suite facilities.
**Gower Hotel**, 129 Sussex Gardens, W2, tel: (020) 7262 2262. Family-run hotel in conveniently located listed building, all rooms with en suite facilities.

## The City, the East End and Docklands
### MID-RANGE
**Barbican Hotel,** 120 Central Street, EC1, tel: (020) 7251 1565. Modern hotel, close to Barbican Arts Centre and City.
**Tower Thistle Hotel**, St Katherine's Way, E1, tel: (020) 7481 2575. Modern; superbly situated next to Tower Bridge.

## North London
### MID-RANGE
**Kandara Guest House**, 68 Ockenden Road, N1, tel: (020) 7226 5721. Small family-run establishment with four shared bathrooms.

## Further afield
### MID-RANGE
**Petersham Hotel**, Nightingale Lane, Richmond tel: (020) 8940 7471. Near Richmond Park; views over the Thames.
**The Windmill**, Clapham Common Southside, tel: (020) 8673 4578. On the edge of Clapham Common, with few competitors; reasonable value.

# London at a Glance

In addition to the ubiquitous fast-food places, London has several good-quality chains with reasonable prices and branches in strategic locations. So look out for: **Café Rouge** (French), **PRET A MANGER** (chemical-free sandwiches and other snacks), **Bella Pasta** (Italian), **Café Flo** (French), **Garfunkel's** (American), **Sofra** (Turkish), **Café Uno** (Italian), **Cork & Bottle** (wine-bars with good food), **Micky's** (mostly outside the centre: proper traditional fish and chips at non-tourist prices) and **cafés in galleries and museums** should not be ignored: many are excellent. There's a detailed Eating Out listing in the weekly magazine *What's On*.

### Whitehall and Westminster
**Tate Britain Restaurant**, Tate Britain, Millbank, SW1, tel: (020) 7887 8877. Spacious, imposing setting, with changing menu and excellent desserts.

### The West End
**Tiddy Dols**, 55 Shepherd Market, W1, tel: (020) 7499 2357. Traditional English food served in quaint Georgian building.
**Gay Hussar**, 2 Greek Street, W1, tel: (020) 7437 0973. Famous and long-established Hungarian restaurant.
**dell'Ugo**, 56 Frith Street, W1, tel: (020) 7734 8300. Inexpensive café on the ground floor and expensive

two-tier restaurant above; Mediterranean fare at this popular Soho spot.
**Hard Rock Café**, 150 Old Park Lane, W1, tel: (020) 7629 0382. Queues are one of the drawbacks of this famous burger joint decorated with rock memorabilia; high prices but usually worth the wait.
**Planet Hollywood**, 13 Coventry St, W1, tel: (020) 7287 1000. This busy theme restaurant serves enormous portions.
**Sports Café**, 80 Haymarket, SW1, tel: (020) 7839 8300. Catch 150 satellite channels on 120 TV sets; restaurant, three bars and a dance floor.
**The Stockpot**, 38 Panton Street, London WC2, tel: (020) 7839 5142. Certainly not *haute cuisine*, but here is possibly the cheapest filling meal in town.
**Kettners**, 29 Romilly Street, W1, tel: (020) 7734 6112. Trendy pizza joint in interesting old building.

### Bloomsbury and Covent Garden
**Simpson's in the Strand**, 100 Strand, WC2, tel: (020) 7836 9112. Very traditional; waiters wheeling out silver platters of beef and the like. Excellent puddings and breakfasts.
**Porters English Restaurant**, 17 Henrietta Street, WC2, tel: (020) 7379 3556. Excellent traditional food in the heart of Covent Garden.

### West and Southwest London
**Bibendum**, Michelin House, 81 Fulham Rd, SW3, tel: (020) 7581 5817. Classy, eclectic cuisine in delightful old Michelin building. Pricey, but worth it.
**Chutney Mary**, 535 King's Rd, SW10, tel: (020) 7351 3113. Best of 'British Raj' cooking and regional Indian dishes.
**La Gavroche**, 43 Upper Brook Street, W1, tel: (020) 7408 0881. One of London's top restaurants, famous for the high standard of its classic French cuisine.
**Kam Tong**, 59–63 Queensway, W2, tel: (020) 7229 6065. Popular, with excellent Cantonese food – in an area offering many other good eating options.

### North London
**Belgo Noord**, 72 Chalk Farm Road, NW1, tel: (020) 7267 0718. Amusing décor; inexpensive and generous portions of Belgian favourites; but book in advance.
**Sea Shell**, 49–51 Lisson Grove, NW1, tel: (020) 7723 8703. Top quality fish-and-chippie.

### South and Southeast London
**Butler's Wharf Chop House**, Butler's Wharf, 36E Shad Thames, SE1, tel: (020) 7403 3403. Fabulous views of Tower Bridge from Terence Conran's riverfront restaurant. Traditional British food at its best.

## London at a Glance

**Le Pont de la Tour**, Butler's Wharf, 36D Shad Thames, SE1, tel: (020) 7403 8403. Another Conran outpost, overlooking the river. Attentive service, exhaustive wine list, accent on seafoods.

### WHERE TO SHOP

Napoleon dubbed the English a 'nation of shopkeepers' and London has something for everyone, whatever your tastes or your budget, from grand department stores to speciality shops or bargain-basement market stalls.
**Opening hours** vary – mostly 09:00/10:00–17:30/19:00 Monday–Saturday, noon to 16:00/18:00 Sunday.
**Late-night shopping** varies from area to area (in Kensington High Street, Oxford Street and Covent Garden it is on Thursdays; in Knightsbridge and Chelsea it's Wednesdays) with shops open until 19:00 or 20:00. Many shops are also open longer hours in the month before Christmas.
Prices are considerably reduced during the two major **sales** periods, with the winter sales – the biggest event – running from just after Christmas until early February, and the summer sales starting in June or July. All the large shops (and most of the smaller ones) accept **credit cards**, as do most other establishments, but **traveller's cheques** are not commonly accepted as a form of payment.
Overseas visitors can sometimes claim back **sales tax** (VAT, or Value Added Tax) on goods purchased (*see* **Money Matters**, p. 122). London has so many hundreds of shops that it would take a whole book to list them all; this rundown covers some of the main shopping areas.

### Oxford Street and Surrounds

Almost a mile long, **Oxford Street** may be one of the most famous shopping streets in the capital but the stretch to the east of Oxford Circus is rather tawdry, filled with tacky souvenir shops and second-rate cut-price clothing. It is the stretch west of Oxford Circus that contains most of the more upmarket establishments and is home to major chains and department stores such as Selfridges, Marks & Spencer, John Lewis, Next, Debenhams and British Home Stores, as well as mega-media stores such as HMV and Virgin.
To the north of Oxford Street, **St Christopher's Place** features numerous designer outlets, whilst on the opposite side **South Molton Street** is another popular area for fashion boutiques. Leading off Oxford Street, **Bond Street** and **New Bond Street** feature quality fashions, haute couture, art galleries, jewellery (including Asprey & Garrard) and antique shops.
Leading down from Oxford Circus to Piccadilly, **Regent Street** is home to Liberty's department store, Laura Ashley, Hamleys toyshop, several crystal and china shops, a Disney store and Warner Brothers, and also classic British clothing shops such as Aquascutum, Jaeger and Austin Reed. To the east of Regent Street, **Carnaby Street** was world famous during the 'Swinging Sixties' but is now full of tacky souvenir shops.
Running parallel to Regent Street on its west side, **Savile Row** is well known as the best place to go for bespoke tailoring.

### Piccadilly and St James's

**Piccadilly Circus** features the indoor shopping complexes of the Trocadero and London Pavilion, as well as Lillywhites, the sports department store, and the massive Tower Records. **Piccadilly** is lined with car showrooms and airline offices but has some famous name shops such as Fortnum and Mason, and Hatchards (books). South of Piccadilly in St James's is **Jermyn Street**, which has numerous small, old-fashioned shops offering exciting finds such as beautiful hand-made shoes, shirts and the like.

# London at a Glance

On the north side of Piccadilly, the **Burlington Arcade** is another old-fashioned enclave with good quality shops selling everything from porcelain to antique jewellery, Irish linen and cashmere jumpers.

### Knightsbridge, Kensington and Chelsea

One of the most expensive shopping areas in the capital, **Knightsbridge** features numerous classy boutiques and designer fashion shops, as well as world-famous Harrods. **Sloane Street**, with Harvey Nichols and yet more expensive clothing outlets, leads down into **Sloane Square** and the beginning of **King's Road**. Once one of London's great fashion meccas, King's Road can still hold its own with plenty of trendy designer outlets. **Kensington** has antique shops along **Kensington Church Street**, department stores and clothes boutiques on **Kensington High Street**, and a cluster of fashionable designer outlets in tiny **Brompton Cross**.

### Covent Garden and Soho

**Covent Garden** has a wonderfully eclectic mix of shops, selling virtually everything from designer clothes to arts, crafts, books, antiques and more. To the north of Covent Garden, **Floral Street** is hot on street fashions, while **Neal's Yard** tends to be the focus for rather 'alternative' goods and wholefoods.

Alongside the pornographic outlets in **Soho** there are many unusual specialist shops, from Continental delicatessens to small record outlets.

Between Soho and Covent Garden, **Charing Cross Road** is synonymous with the book trade, with numerous specialized outlets (for both new and secondhand books), and major bookstores such as Foyle (No. 119) and Waterstones (No. 121).

## MARKETS

London has a vast range of markets, rewarding places to browse for crafts, antiques, and bargains of every description among the hordes. Some of the better known ones include **Brick Lane** market (open Sundays 08:00–13:00 near Spitalfields E1); the **Camden Lock Market**, Camden Passage (*see* p. 91); **Portobello Road** (fruit and vegetables, clothes, antiques, records; open 10:00–18:00 Saturdays); **Greenwich** (bric-a-brac, arts, crafts, clothes; open 09:30–17:00 Wednesday, Friday, Sunday); and **Petticoat Lane** (clothes, bric-a-brac, and more; open 09:00–14:00 Sunday, 09:00–15:00, Monday–Friday).

## DEPARTMENT STORES

**Fortnum and Mason**, 181 Piccadilly, W1, tel: (020) 7734 8040. Open 10:00–18:30, Mon–Sat.

**Harrods**, 87 Brompton Road, SW1, tel: (020) 7730 1234. Open 10:00–19:00, Mon–Sat.

**Harvey Nichols**, 102–125 Knightsbridge, SW1, tel: (020) 7235 5000. Open 10:00–19:00, Mon, Tues, Sat; 10:00–20:00, Wed–Fri.

**John Lewis**, 278–306 Oxford Street, W1, tel: (020) 7629 7711. Open 09:30–18:00, Mon, Tues, Wed, Fri; 10:00–20:00 Thurs; 09:00–18:00 Sat.

**Liberty**, 212–299 Regent Street, W1, tel: (020) 7734 1234. Open 10:00–18:30 Mon–Wed and Fri–Sat; 10:00–20:00 Thurs.

**Marks & Spencer**, 458 Oxford Street, W1, tel: (020) 7935 7954. Open 09:00–20:00, Mon–Fri; 09:00–19:00 Sat; 12:00–18:00 Sun.

**Selfridges**, 400 Oxford Street, W1, tel: (020) 7629 1234. Open 10:00–19:00 Mon–Wed, and 10:00–20:00 Thurs and Fri; 09:30–19:00 Sat; and 12:00–18:00 Sun.

## TOURS AND EXCURSIONS

One of the greatest advantages of visiting London is that there are so many other interesting places within a reasonable distance of the capital which you can

# London at a Glance

visit for an enjoyable day out, or even for a slightly longer stay. With frequent train services from the eight main rail termini in central London you don't have to worry about driving either; coaches are another option, with hundreds of services from the Victoria Coach Station daily. **Victoria Coach Station**, 164 Buckingham Palace Road, SW1, tel: (020) 7730 3466. The following tour operators offer day-tours from London to all the major tourist destinations, and all use qualified Blue Badge Guides:

**Golden Tours**,
(020) 7233 7030.

**Evan Evans**,
(020) 7950 1777.

**Frames Rickards**,
(020) 7837 3111.

**Hallam Anderson Tours**,
(020) 7234 0505.

To the southeast of London, **Canterbury** has long been a place of pilgrimage, with the focal point being the city's magnificent cathedral. The vibrant Sussex coastal town of **Brighton** has a distinguished Regency heritage, excellent shopping and a traditional English seaside pier; the highlight is the refurbished Royal Pavilion, the seaside palace of George IV.
The coastline of Central Southern England features numerous popular seaside resorts as well as the historic naval port of **Portsmouth**. Further inland are the ancient cathedral cities of **Winchester** and **Salisbury**. Near Salisbury, the monoliths of **Stonehenge** are one of the country's most famous prehistoric monuments. The West Country features numerous picturesque villages, stately homes and historic monuments. In the county of Avon, **Bath** was first popularized by the Romans as a spa town and with its fine Georgian architecture is considered one of the most elegant towns in the country (it has good shops, too).
To the north of Bath, the **Cotswolds** are famous for their pretty, honey-coloured sandstone villages set amongst rolling hills. One of the finest medieval castles in the country is to be found at **Warwick**, to the north of the Cotswolds, while nearby **Stratford-upon-Avon** is, of course, the much-visited birthplace of the father of theatre, William Shakespeare. Central England is home to the ancient university town of **Oxford**, where many of the graceful college buildings are open to the public. Further east, the rival university town of **Cambridge** also boasts many fine buildings which can be explored by punt along the river or on foot.

USEFUL CONTACTS

**London Regional Transport** (LRT) enquiry service for the underground and buses, tel: (020) 7222 1234 (24 hours, 7 days). LRT recorded travel information: tel: (020) 7222 1200.
**National train enquiries**, tel: (08457) 48 49 50.
**National Express** (coach service), tel: (08705) 80 80 80.
**Heathrow airport**, tel: (08700) 000 123.
**Gatwick airport**, tel: (01293) 53 53 53.
**London City airport**, tel: (020) 7646 0088.
**Stansted airport**, tel: (01279) 680 500.
**Airbus service** (to Heathrow), tel: (020) 7222 1234.
**Victoria Coach station**, tel: (020) 7730 3466.
**Docklands Light Railway**, tel: (020) 7363 9898.
**Computer Taxis** 24-hour black cabs, tel: (020) 7286 0286.
**Public Carriage Office**, tel: (020) 7230 1631 (for complaints about the taxis); tel: (020) 7833 0996 (for property lost in taxis).
**Car Rental:**
**Avis**, tel: (0870) 590 0500.
**Hertz**, tel: (020) 8679 1799.
**Europcar**, tel: (0345) 222 525.
**Hire for Lower**, tel: (020) 7491 1111.
**Disabled:** Artsline (free information on access to all arts and entertainment venues and events), tel: (020) 7388 2227.

# London at a Glance

**Holiday Care Service** (advisory service on accommodation for the disabled), tel: (01293) 774 535.
**LRT Unit for Disabled Passengers** (details on access to transport services), tel: (020) 7918 3312.

**The London Tourist Board** does not run a telephone enquiry service, but there is an automated information service, Visitorcall, with different lines (updated daily) providing information on What's On, Out & About, Where to Take Children, Theatre, Places to Visit, Accommodation, etc. For a free card listing all services, tel: (020) 7971 0026.
**London weather forecast**, tel: (09062) 500 951.
**Events listings by fax:**
**Major events** (12 pages), tel: (09068) 353 715.
**Events in London**, tel: (09068) 353 716.
All the above LTB numbers are premium rate lines: calls cost 60p per minute.

**Double-decker hop-on hop-off sightseeing tours**
These are an excellent introduction to London, providing masses of background information and a variety of special offers, including tickets for some attractions that enable you to queue-jump. Tickets are valid for 24 hours and you can get on and off at any stop. The three main companies all have frequent services and stops that are convenient for the sights. Most vehicles have open top decks. **Big Bus**, tel: (020) 7233 9533; **London Pride**, tel: (020) 7520 2050; **Original London**, tel: (020) 8877 1722.

**Driver Guides:**
• Flexible itineraries tailored to your interests and personalized service are among the advantages of a driver-guided tour.
• **Black Taxi Tours of London**, tel: (020) 7289 4371.
• **British Tours**, tel: (020) 7734 8734.
• **Take a Guide**, tel: (020) 8960 0459.

**Guide Booking Agencies:**
The London registered guides have all undertaken a rigorous training course, after which they are issued with the coveted Blue Badge and photo-card licence. The companies listed below can book Blue Badge guides for anything from general sightseeing to special interest tours:
• **Professional Guide Services**, tel: (020) 8874 2745.

• **Tours Guides Ltd**, tel: (020) 7495 5504.

**Walking Tours:**
• **Historical Tours**. Daily programme of guided walks on a cultural theme, tel: (020) 8668 4019.
• **Mystery Walks**. Focuses on the East End of London and popular 'Jack the Ripper' walks, tel: (020) 8558 9446.
• **Original London Walks**. London's oldest established walking tour company, which features a varied programme of over 40 walks on different themes, tel: (020) 7624 3978.
• **Zigzag Audio Tours**. A choice of five self-guided audio tours in six languages; tel: (020) 8458 5310, e-mail: info@zigzagtours.com website: www.zigzagtours.com

**River/Canal Boat Operators:**
• **Bateaux London**, tel: (020) 7925 2215.
• **Catamaran Cruises**, tel: (020) 7987 1185.
• **Westminster Passenger Service** (upriver), tel: (020) 7930 2062.
• **Jason's Canal Boat**, tel: (020) 7286 3428.

| LONDON | J | F | M | A | M | J | J | A | S | O | N | D |
|---|---|---|---|---|---|---|---|---|---|---|---|---|
| AVERAGE TEMP. °F | 40 | 40 | 44 | 49 | 55 | 61 | 64 | 64 | 59 | 52 | 46 | 42 |
| AVERAGE TEMP. °C | 5 | 5 | 7 | 10 | 13 | 16 | 18 | 18 | 15 | 12 | 8 | 6 |
| HOURS OF SUN DAILY | 1.5 | 2.2 | 3.7 | 5.3 | 6.6 | 7.1 | 6.6 | 6.2 | 4.7 | 3.2 | 1.7 | 1.3 |
| RAINFALL ins. | 2.1 | 1.6 | 1.5 | 1.5 | 1.8 | 1.8 | 2.2 | 2.3 | 1.9 | 2.2 | 3 | 1.9 |
| RAINFALL mm | 54 | 40 | 37 | 37 | 46 | 45 | 57 | 59 | 49 | 57 | 64 | 48 |
| DAYS OF RAINFALL | 15 | 13 | 11 | 12 | 12 | 11 | 12 | 11 | 13 | 13 | 15 | 15 |

# Travel Tips

## Tourist Information

Overseas offices of the **British Tourist Authority** (BTA) have a range of leaflets, brochures, free maps and guides, and events calendars. Offices can be found in Australia (Sydney), Canada (Mississauga), Ireland (Dublin), New Zealand (Auckland), South Africa (Sandton), Singapore, and the USA (New York, LA and Chicago). Main tourist offices within London are the **British Visitor Centre** at 1 Lower Regent Street, SW1, open 09:30–18:30, Mon–Fri; 09:00–17:00, Sat–Sun (10:00–16:00, Nov–May), and the **London Tourist Board** (LTB) at Victoria Station (open 08:00–21:00, Mon–Sat; 08:00–18:00 Sun, reduced hours in winter); website: www.londontown.com Neither centre accepts telephone enquiries. LTB desks are located at **Heathrow Airport** Terminal 3 concourse open daily 06:00–23:00; tube stations in Terminals 1, 2 and 3 open daily 08:00–18:00 (till 19:00 June–Sept), Liverpool Street Station tube, open daily 08:00–18:00 (till 19:00 June–Sept) and Waterloo Eurostar Terminal, open daily 08:30–22:30. There are centres providing comprehensive information about their immediate areas: in the City (see p. 73), Southwark (see p. 99) and Greenwich (see p. 102).

## Entry Requirements

No visas required for travellers from the USA, Japan, Iceland, Austria, Finland, Switzerland, and the European Union countries. Citizens of Canada, Australia, New Zealand and most Commonwealth countries (exceptions include Sri Lanka, Nigeria, Bangladesh, Ghana, India, Pakistan and Nepal) are also not required to have visas. The nationals of other countries should check.

## Customs

For goods bought outside the EU, these restrictions on tax- and duty-free goods apply:
• 200 cigarettes, or 100 cigarillos, or 50 cigars, or 250g (8 ounces) tobacco.
• 2 litres (4 pints) still table wine plus 1 litre (2 pints) spirits or liqueur (over 22% proof), or 2 litres (4 pints) of fortified or sparkling wine (under 22% proof).
• 60ml (2 fluid ounces) perfume plus 250ml (8 fluid ounces) of toilet water.
• Other goods valued to £145. Restrictions apply on the import of other items (firearms, protected species, meat products, etc) and pets. There are no restrictions on currency.

## Health Requirements

No vaccinations are required.

## Money Matters

**Currency:** British currency is the pound sterling (£), divided into 100 pence (p). Coin denominations are 1p, 2p, 5p, 10p, 20p, 50p, £1 and £2. Notes are in denominations of £5, £10, £20, £50.

**Banks:** The four major banks, with branches throughout the city are: National Westminster, Barclays, Lloyds and HSBC. Standard opening hours are 09:30–17:00, Mon–Fri, but there are variations. Some branches open for a few hours on Sat.

**Currency Exchange: Traveller's cheques:** You'll need your passport when cashing traveller's cheques. Commission is usually

charged. Banks offer the best rates, but numerous **bureaux de change** work longer hours.
**Credit cards:** Most hotels, shops and restaurants accept international credit cards.
**VAT:** Consumer goods (with major exceptions such as food and books) are subject to a 17.5% sales tax known as VAT (Value Added Tax). Visitors from non-EU countries can re-coup VAT on major items but, before you buy, ask for the appropriate form. Customs will validate this when leaving.
**Tipping:** Service charges are usually included in bills, but many restaurants may also leave a blank space on credit card counterfoils to encourage customers to tip twice! If a tip is not included, waiters expect 10–15%. Hairdressers and taxis expect a tip of about 10%. Don't tip if service has been poor. Bar staff (but not in pubs) may also expect a tip.

## Accommodation

London has many options, ranging from the **deluxe** to homely **bed and breakfasts** (B&Bs), **hostels** and **budget hotels**. Even in the peak summer season there is rarely a shortage of places to stay but the problem is one of cost: London is an expensive city, and this is more than reflected in the price of hotel rooms.
**Accommodation agencies:** The **London Tourist Board** have over 1000 hotels and other accommodation on their books within a 20km radius of the capital. The booking fee is £5, and a deposit is deducted from your hotel bill. Reserva-

---

| PUBLIC HOLIDAYS |
| :---: |
| **1 January •** |
| New Year's Day |
| **Late March/early April •** |
| Good Friday and |
| Easter Monday |
| **First Monday in May •** |
| May Day Holiday |
| **Last Monday in May •** |
| Spring Bank Holiday |
| **Last Monday in August •** |
| Summer Bank Holiday |
| **25 December •** |
| Christmas Day |
| **26 December •** |
| Boxing Day |

tions at LTB centres (*see* p. 122) or by credit card, tel: (020) 7932 2020.
**British Hotels Reservation Centres** (BHRC) have branches at Heathrow, Gatwick and City airports, Victoria and Waterloo rail stations and Victoria coach station. Bookings are free. Tel: (020) 7604 2890.
**Hotels and B&Bs:** Hotels classified by stars and all other types of accommodation by diamonds (both 1–5), with ratings depending on quality and range of facilities. These determine categories but give no indication of character or style. Establishments with 4 or more rooms are required to display notices of charges, and whether this includes break-fast, service charges, VAT, etc. In the off-peak winter season, negotiate a discount if you're staying for several days, but bargaining is not the norm. Many upmarket hotels offer special weekend rates to fill rooms usually occupied by weekday business guests, so

look into these mini-packages if you want to treat yourself to a weekend in a smart hotel. Most of the top hotels are centred around Knightsbridge, Mayfair and Belgravia. A double room in the famous Dorchester or Claridges will cost £300+ per night, with a level of service commensurate with the price. International chains catering for business clients, such as the Hilton, Inter-Continental and Marriott are in a similar bracket.
**Bed and Breakfasts** are a relative bargain in price terms; charges in central areas are seasonal, about £60/80 for a double room including a tradi-tional English breakfast – if you don't mind travelling into the city every day you can find them cheaper (£30/50) in out-lying suburbs.
**Self-catering apartments** can offer good value for fami-lies, starting at about £150 a week (up to ten times that!); the London Tourist Board can advise on what's available.

## Eating Out

London restaurants cater to every taste and budget – the diversity is almost unmatched by any other capital city. Even traditional **British** cooking, once a by-word for stodgy food, has been revitalized by a new generation of chefs and can now hold its own against the classic cuisines. **French**, **Italian** and **Greek** restaurants are all fairly common, and have recently been joined by the spread of **Spanish** tapas and innumerable **Thai** restaurants. Britain has long been known for its ethnic foods, particularly **Chinese** and **Indian**; **Turkish**, **Malaysian** and **Lebanese** restaurants are found in abundance and most national cuisines are represented.

In recent years **pub** food has improved enormously, and while it may be hard to find a freshly made sandwich in some areas, in others the range and quality of bar food is as good as some restaurants. There are also a number of **bistros** and **wine bars**, where as well as sampling a range of fine wines you can find salads, light meals, and other fare. If all else fails, a simple **café** or **tea-room** can provide snacks, sandwiches or a quick meal.

## Transport

London Underground and London Buses operate a 24hr telephone service for travel information, tel: (020) 7222 1234. **Travel Information Centres** can provide useful free leaflets and pocket maps on bus and tube services; they are located at Oxford Circus, Piccadilly Circus, Hammersmith and St James's Park tube stations and at Euston, Victoria, Paddington, King's Cross and Liverpool Street mainline stations, as well as in all four terminals at Heathrow Airport.

If you're planning on using public transport extensively during the course of a day it's worth investing in a **Travelcard**, valid during off-peak times only (from 09:30 weekdays, all day at weekends) but good value compared to individual tickets (a one-day travelcard is £3.90 for two zones,

which compares to single-journey tube tickets of £1.50 in zone 1, £1.80 for zones 1 & 2, and £3.50 for all zones). Travelcards can be used on tubes, most buses and Docklands Light Railway. There are also weekly travelcards (photo required) and carnets: books of 10 tube tickets.

Buses are cheaper than tubes, a fact reflected in the cost of bus passes: £11.50 (7 days) or £3 (1 day), compared with a flat rate of £1 per bus in the centre. Night buses (designated N), Airbuses and travel before 09:30 are excluded from passes and travelcards.

## Business Hours

Most **shops** are open 09:30–17:30, Mon–Sat, although different areas have their own late-night shopping days (Wednesdays in Knightsbridge, Thursday in Oxford Street, etc). Large supermarket chains stay open very late (some for 24 hours) Mon–Sat, and small corner shops (similar to convenience stores) stay open until 22:00 or later. Sunday trading is now firmly established in London, with

supermarkets and many department stores open 12:00–16:00.

**Office** hours are usually 09:30–17:30, Mon–Fri (for **banks** *see* under **Money Matters**, p. 122). Office workers usually have a lunch break between 13:00–14:00. Opening hours of **Museums** and **tourist attractions** vary enormously, but most are open daily by 10:00 and close 17:30–18:30, with shorter hours on Sundays. Virtually everything stops on **Christmas Day** (including transport), but most establishments treat other public holidays (known as bank holidays) as Sundays.

## Time

During the winter Britain is on **Greenwich Mean Time** (GMT), and during the summer (from March to October) on **British Summer Time** (BST) which is one hour ahead of GMT.
**Europe:**
GMT plus 1hr.
**USA, Canada (East):**
GMT minus 5hrs.
**USA, Canada (West):**
GMT minus 8hrs.

| CONVERSION CHART | | |
|---|---|---|
| **From** | **To** | **Multiply By** |
| Millimetres | Inches | 0.0394 |
| Metres | Yards | 1.0936 |
| Metres | Feet | 3.281 |
| Kilometres | Miles | 0.6214 |
| Kilometres square | Square miles | 0.386 |
| Hectares | Acres | 2.471 |
| Litres | Pints | 1.760 |
| Kilograms | Pounds | 2.205 |
| Tonnes | Tons | 0.984 |
| To convert Celsius to Fahrenheit: x 9 ÷ 5 + 32 | | |

**Australia:**
GMT plus 8–10hrs.
**New Zealand:**
GMT plus 12hrs.
**South Africa:**
GMT plus 2hrs.

## Communications

**Post:** Post offices are generally open 09:00–17:30, Mon–Fri; 09:00–12:30 or 13:00, Sat. The Trafalgar Square Post Office (24–28 William IV St) is open 08:00–20:00, Mon–Thurs; 08:30–20:00 Fri, 09:00–20:00 Sat. **Postage stamps** can be bought at post office counters, from vending machines, and in many newsagents.
**Telephones:** Public **payphones** are operated by British Telecom (BT) and are either coin-operated or, increasingly, card-operated: **phonecards** are available from post offices and newsagents and come in denominations of £3, £5, £10 and £20. Some payphones also accept credit cards.
London's area code has recently changed to '020', with the actual number increasing from 7 to 8 digits. If you have old listings, use '020-7' in place of '0171' and '020-8' in place of '0181'. When calling within London, you need only the 8-digit number that begins with '7' or '8'.
Any number beginning '09' is premium rate (up to 60p a minute) and numbers beginning '07' are mobiles (expensive). '0800' and '0808' are free lines. Try not to use the telephone in your **hotel** room: mark-ups are among the world's highest. To make

an international call, dial 00, followed by the country code and then the area code:
**Australia** 61
**USA & Canada** 1
**Ireland** 353
**New Zealand** 64
**France** 33
**Singapore** 65
**Hong Kong** 852
**South Africa** 27

**Operator assistance** 100
**International Operator** 155
**Directory assistance** 192
**International directory assistance** 153

---

### GOOD READING

• Duncan, Andrew (1995) *Secret London.* New Holland, London. Explores little-known and hidden facets of the capital, with 20 miles of walks.
• Duncan, Andrew (1991) *Walking London.* New Holland, London. Features 30 original walks in and around the capital.
• Porter, Roy. *London: A Social History.* Hamish Hamilton. Engaging and comprehensive account of the capital's development.
• Tames, Richard (1992) *Traveller's History of London.* Windrush Press. A lively and compact account of the capital's history, from Londinium to Docklands.
• Hamilton, Patrick. *20,000 Streets Under the Sky.* Hogarth/Trafalgar. Romantic trilogy set in the sleazy Soho of the 1930s.

---

## Electricity

The current is 240 volts AC (50 Hz). Most American or European appliances will need an adaptor (ask your hotel if they can lend you one, otherwise try a pharmacist or an electrical shop).

## Weights and Measures

The imperial system of measurements has officially been replaced by the metric system, and that is used in shops, etc. (sometimes in tandem with imperial), but imperial is still common in speech.

## Health Precautions

No special health precautions are necessary. Most European countries (and some in the Commonwealth) have reciprocal health arrangements should you need treatment at an NHS hospital; you will need to obtain the relevant forms before you leave home. For other nationalities, accident and emergency care is generally free at NHS hospitals' casualty departments, but other medical treatment (including hospitalization) will be charged for. It's therefore advisable to arrange comprehensive travel insurance before you leave home.

## Personal Safety

Compared to many cities, London is a relatively safe destination and the greatest risk is from thieves and pickpockets hanging around busy shopping streets or on crowded underground platforms or trains. Use common sense.

• Don't carry more cash than you will need for the day.

• Keep your wallet or purse out of sight; keep handbags fastened and don't carry a wallet in your back pocket.

• Never leave a handbag, suitcase, or coat unattended.

• Avoid poorly lit, quiet areas (such as parks) after dark. If you are subject to a mugging or robbery, report it to the local police station (see under 'Police' in the phone book or call Directory Enquiries on 192).

## Emergencies

The familiar image of the British 'bobby' plodding the streets endures, although they are an increasingly rare sight as patrol cars now dominate. Nevertheless, the police are generally approachable and helpful should you be lost or in trouble. In an emergency for police, fire or ambulance dial 999 or 112.

## Disabled Access

Contact Transport for London Access & Mobility, Windsor House, 50 Victoria St, London SW1H 0TL, tel: (020) 7941 4600. Open 09:00–17:00, Mon–Fri.

## Etiquette

London tends to be an easy-going place with very few formal dress codes or similar restrictions. A night at the opera or in a really top-class restaurant will, of course, necessitate more formal wear, but otherwise smart, casual clothes will do almost everywhere. The British are inveterate believers in **queueing**,

---

### FESTIVALS AND EVENTS

**Late Jan/early Feb** • Chinese New Year
**March** • Ideal Home Exhibition, Chelsea Antiques Fair
**Late March/early April** •
Oxford v Cambridge Boat Race
**April** • Flora London Marathon
**May** • Chelsea Flower Show
Royal Windsor Horse Show
**June** • Trooping the Colour
Royal Academy Summer Exhibition (runs till Aug)
Derby Day
Royal Ascot
Biggin Hill Air Fair
**Late June/early July** • Henley Regatta
Wimbledon Lawn Tennis Championships
**July** • Farnborough Air Display
Kenwood Lakeside Concerts (run till Aug)
City of London Festival
Henry Wood Promenade Concerts (run till Sept)
**August** • Great British Beer Festival
Notting Hill Carnival
**September** • Chelsea Antiques Fair
**Late Sept/early Oct** • Horse of the Year Show
Costermongers Harvest Festival
**November** • Lord Mayor's Show
London to Brighton Veteran Car Rally
Guy Fawkes Night
State Opening of Parliament
Festival of Remembrance
**December** • International Showjumping

For a full rundown on special occasions get the *London Events* booklet from the London Tourist Board. To check the current events, consult the weekly listings magazines *Time Out* and *What's On* or the daily *Evening Standard*.

---

whether it be at a bus stop, in shops or elsewhere, and don't take kindly to those not prepared to stand in line for their turn. The exception is during the rush hour on tubes, buses and trains, when a free-for-all is more likely to prevail. On the Underground you stand on the right on escalators, and keep the left clear. In recent years **smoking** has become less acceptable in public places and is now totally banned on all **public transport** and in most public buildings. Restaurants and some hotels are now also increasingly anti-smoking: check before booking.